HEALING: GOD'S WORK AMONG US

Healing: God's Work Among Us

John Bertolucci
with
Nick Cavnar

SERVANT BOOKS
Ann Arbor, Michigan

Cover design by Gerald Gawronski
Cover photo by Ed Cooper

Published by Servant Books
P.O. Box 8617
Ann Arbor, Michigan 48107

Printed in the United States of America
ISBN 0-89283-351-3

87 88 89 90 91 92   10 9 8 7 6 5 4 3 2 1

Contents

ONE

Healing Does Happen

THE MESSAGE ON MY HOTEL ROOM DOOR SAID only "Emergency," with a name and phone number. The name seemed distantly familiar.

"Who is it, Lord?" I wondered as I opened the door and went to the phone. Then I remembered: Brian had been a student in a high school class I taught nearly twenty years before. I hadn't heard from him since.

It was late Friday night, and I was in Detroit to preach at a big evangelistic rally scheduled for the next day. The leadership meeting preceding the rally had just ended; I was tired and ready for bed. And here was a message from someone I hadn't seen for twenty years.

"Emergency room," answered an operator when I dialed the number. I had reached a hospital in my home diocese of Albany, New York. I asked for Brian and was told he was in critical condition and could not take calls. I explained that I was a priest: could I speak to a relative?

After a couple of minutes another voice came on the line—a member of Brian's family.

"This is Fr. John Bertolucci," I said. "I am calling from Detroit. I have a message here about Brian. What's happening?"

"Father, Brian's dying."

My former student had a growth on his lung, I learned. His condition had become critical, and he was not expected to survive much longer.

"Brian keeps asking for you, Father," the relative explained. "That's why we called. Can you come to him?"

"What should I do, Lord?" I whispered. I was scheduled for an all-day rally the next day; then I would return to Steubenville and leave almost immediately for an important conference in Rome. None of my travels would take me anywhere near Albany and the hospital where Brian lay dying.

I explained my situation to Brian's relative.

"I understand, Father," she said. "All I can say is that he's dying and he keeps asking for you."

I prayed silently again for a minute. What should I do? With my whole heart I yearned to be at the bedside of the young man who was calling for my help. I did not feel God wanted me to neglect my other commitments, but somehow I had to minister to this young man.

"Okay," I told her, "get a piece of paper. I'm going to dictate a prayer, and I want you to go to Brian and lead him in this prayer. Ask him to mean every word with his heart. Tell him that I cannot be there in person, but I'll be standing alongside him spiritually, praying with him."

Then Brian's mother came to the phone. I ministered to her, asking the Lord to control her anxiety, to give her strength, to protect her from panic and fear. I made sure she was right with God, that she had received the Lord Jesus Christ into her life, that she was open to the Holy Spirit and the Lord's healing power.

I spoke with her too about the importance of the sacramental ministry—making sure that Brian had the opportunity for confession and the Anointing of the Sick. I wanted to be sure to recommend the right priest, so I prayed for the Lord's guidance. The name of a priest in their area came to mind.

For an hour there in my hotel room in Detroit, I ministered over the phone to this family in Albany. As we prayed, I felt more and more clearly that the Lord was telling us not to despair but to have faith that he would heal Brian. So that was how we prayed, Brian's mother and the other relative and I: separated by miles, yet side-by-side in spirit, interceding before the Father for the healing of this young man.

The next day brought the rally, and then on Sunday I returned to Steubenville to prepare for my trip to Rome. That evening my phone rang. When I answered I heard the unmistakable sound of pumps, the beep of monitors, and the gasping voice of a young man I had not talked to since 1967.

"Father John," Brian gasped. "I prayed the prayer. You *must* pray with me. Can you come?"

Again my heart was torn. I prayed quickly—desperately—for guidance. Again it seemed clear that God did not want me to break my other commitments. Yet I could still minister to Brian, as I had ministered to his mother, by phone.

"Brian," I said, "We *are* going to pray together—right now."

We prayed for fifteen or twenty minutes, right there over the phone. I encouraged Brian to surrender his life to the Lord, to repent, to turn away from sin, to put aside all the confusion in his mind and heart and let God minister to him. I urged him to talk freely and openly with the chaplain who would be coming.

Brian's voice was peaceful and calm as we finished.

"Will you keep praying for me, Father?" he asked.

"Brian," I promised, "I will pray for you every day I am gone. And I'll see you when I get back from Rome."

The next day on the plane, I thought and prayed a lot about Brian. I felt a strong conviction that God was indeed going to heal him—yet I had doubts too. Medically there was no hope for him. Had my final promise been rash? Would he really still be alive when I returned home?

"Lord," I whispered, "I believe you want to heal Brian, and I claim that promise for him. But I'm weak, Lord, and my faith is weak. Help my lack of trust!"

I was in Rome for a month, and every day I remembered Brian in my prayers. I planned to call him soon after I returned home. But my first night back at the monastery in Steubenville, it hit me like a ton of bricks: "Call Brian's hospital—*now!*"

It felt odd to be calling for someone without knowing for sure if he was even still alive.

"I'm calling about Brian," I told the hospital operator. "Is he . . . ? Did he . . . ?"

"Do you want to talk to him?" the puzzled operator asked.

"*Can* I talk to him?"

"Sure." She sounded so matter of fact, while I was about to hit the ceiling with sheer joy. "He's upstairs in a private room. I'll ring."

A strong, healthy voice answered. Brian!

"Brian, how are you?"

"Father John, I'm well! I'm getting discharged in two days!"

Brian told me the whole story of what had happened after our long-distance prayer session. The priest I recommended had come to anoint him, hear his confession, and give him absolution and the Eucharist. Later Brian began to feel that he was slipping away, falling. Then suddenly he had a feeling of being pulled back and raised up. From that point, the doctors told him later, he had taken a dramatic turn for the better. Within days his condition had changed completely.

"It's funny," he told me. "The doctors and the nurses are befuddled by the whole thing. Praise God!"

As I hung up the phone, exulting in God's goodness and mercy, I had to ask myself, How would I have ministered to Brian if all this had happened twenty years ago, when I knew him as a high school student?

As a priest of the Catholic church, I would of course have been able to minister the sacraments: to reconcile Brian with God through absolution for his sins, to strengthen him through the Holy Eucharist, to anoint him with consecrated oil and pray the church's official prayers for healing. Through the great power of the sacraments, God could still have intervened to raise Brian up from death.

But certainly, twenty years ago, I would not have expected that to happen. If the doctors had told me that Brian was dying, I would have gone to his hospital room only to prepare him and his family for his death. Nothing would have surprised me more than to see him recover in answer to my prayers.

In my earlier book, *On Fire with the Spirit,* I told of the event that changed my personal life and my priestly ministry. On St. Valentine's Day in 1969, through the prayers of a small Catholic prayer group meeting in the living room of a suburban home in Glenville, New York, I encountered Jesus Christ as a living, personal Savior and Lord. I experienced his Holy Spirit pouring into me with power, strength, fervor, and love. The preaching ministry with which I serve the church, my life at the Franciscan Monastery of the Holy Spirit in Steubenville, my television program, *The Glory of God*—all these things have grown from that moment when I came to experience Jesus personally and was baptized in his Holy Spirit.

Along with the many other things that have changed in my life since that night in 1969, I have come to a new understanding of sickness and of healing. I realize today that God is not only able but eager to intervene directly in our lives and restore us to health when we are sick. Healing was part of Jesus' ministry, healing was part of the life of the apostolic church, and healing is still available to God's people today.

The last fifteen years have seen a great renewal of the healing ministry in the Catholic church and in many other churches. Thousands of people attend healing services led by priests like Fr. Ralph DiOrio, Fr. Edward McDonough, and Fr. Dennis Kelleher. Many religious and laypeople have special healing ministries as well. There are Christian doctors who now include prayer for healing as part of their care for the sick.

There are many, many ordinary people who now have greater faith that God can and will heal them.

I have been privileged to be a part of this renewal, and I have learned much from my brothers and sisters in it. Through their experiences and my own experiences, through prayer and my study of Sacred Scripture and the church's teaching, I have learned to minister to the sick with faith that God will indeed heal. I have seen many healings as a result, and have experienced healing myself. I have come to believe that the charismatic gifts of healing and miracles are to be a normal part of the church's life.

Yet there is another aspect of the healing ministry. While I have seen many healings in the years since 1969, I have also ministered to many suffering people who were not physically healed.

This remains a great puzzle and even an obstacle to faith for many in the healing ministry. Why is it that some are not healed? Why is it that at a healing service where someone is raised up from a wheelchair able to walk, others will leave still in their wheelchairs? Why will one person experience God's deliverance from a terrible disease like cancer, while another, who prays with the same faith, will suffer and die?

Our Christian understanding of sickness and death must include those who are not healed as well as those who are. How do we see God's hand and experience God's help when our prayers for his healing seem to go unanswered?

Some of the most profound memories of my priesthood center around another young man whom I knew during the years I was privileged to serve as pastor of St. Joseph Parish in Little Falls, New York. John was a big, strapping fellow who had been a football star in high school. He was married to a beautiful young woman, and they had one child—a baby girl. But John was also suffering from Lou Gehrig's disease, a fatal paralysis named for the 1930's baseball star who was killed by it.

I visited John regularly, and watched the disease spread through his body. By the end he was totally helpless, paralyzed from the neck down. He whispered to me once—for he could no longer speak aloud—"Do you know what hurts most, Father? Not being able to hold my little girl." So his wife and I put the baby on her daddy's chest, and wrapped his lifeless arms around her and held them there, so he could know that joy again.

I cannot tell you how many times I prayed for John's healing. He and his wife were strong, dedicated Christians, and their home was always filled with faith and love for God. In John's final days the Lord's name was almost constantly on his lips. He whispered over and over, "Jesus, I love you."

In John I saw that God does not always heal disease, even when we pray with faith. I cannot agree with those Christians who maintain that God will always heal, so long as we have sufficient faith. Such teaching places a tremendous burden of guilt upon those whose prayers for healing are not answered. It leads to a strange kind of deception: people cover up any doubts and fears they may feel, as if they could fool God into thinking they have more perfect confidence than they really do.

Spiritual gymnastics of that kind have very little to do with real faith for healing. It is people like John who have taught me the most about faith in God's victory over sickness—people who did not experience physical healing but whose faith and love grew steadily stronger as God sustained them through suffering and death.

Faith for healing, faith in suffering: we do not have to see these as contradictory. I believe that they are both important in a Christian understanding of sickness. In this book we will reflect on both, as we look at the biblical teachings about illness and about God's plan to remove illness from our midst.

Scripture and our church's teaching and traditions do have a great deal to teach us about the reality of sickness and how we are to respond to it. And it begins with perhaps the most basic question of all: Why does sickness even exist?

TWO

Don't Blame God

"WHY IS GOD DOING THIS TO ME? Why is he making me suffer?"

When people get sick, they naturally seem to blame God. Even people who don't believe in God blame him. Those who do believe wonder why the God they love so much wants them to suffer. People may believe that they are being punished or that they have to endure a lot of pain to become better people. They may simply decide that God is capricious and cruel. One way or another, almost everyone seems convinced that sickness and suffering come straight from God.

Is that really what our faith teaches? Does the Bible show us a God who likes to go around striking people with afflictions?

As an ordained minister of the gospel, I have served many people who were undergoing sickness and affliction and suffering, people who were struggling with the *why* of their pain. I have counseled them, I have searched the Scriptures and the church's wisdom for answers to their questions. One thing has become ever clearer to me: Sickness is not God's doing. From the very start, it was not his idea or his intention for any of his people to suffer affliction.

We see this so clearly in the story of the beginnings of the human race. The book of Genesis, we know, was not written as a scientific account of how the universe was formed and how the human race appeared on earth. But Genesis does record the divinely inspired truth about God's plan and original intention for human life. The picture that emerges is something quite different from a God who wants people to suffer.

> The Lord God formed man out of the clay of the ground and blew into his nostrils the breath of life, and so man became a living being. Then the Lord God planted a garden in Eden, in the east, and he placed there the man whom he had formed. Out of the ground the Lord God made various trees grow that were delightful to look at and good for food, with the tree of life in the middle of the garden and the tree of the knowledge of good and bad. . . . The Lord God then took the man and settled him in the garden of Eden, to cultivate and care for it. (Gn 2:7-9, 15)

Genesis goes on to describe the creation of woman, as "a suitable partner" for man, out of God's concern that "it is not good for the man to be alone" (Gn 2:18). Everything in this account speaks to us of God's desire to delight the man and woman he created. He made them to be satisfied, happy, wholesome, balanced, healthy, alive. God desired to provide everything his people needed for happiness.

What went wrong, of course, was that the man and woman rebelled. They wanted to be independent of God; they were tempted with the promise, "You will be like gods" (Gn 3:5). The Bible describes their rebellion through the story of the fruit of the tree that gave knowledge of good and bad. To our own day, that remains the great temptation: to reject God's law and God's definition of good and bad, and instead choose good and evil for ourselves.

I believe that is where sickness entered the world—along with every other form of anguish and heartache and grief and affliction. Sickness began as a consequence of sin, as the result of our first parents' rejecting their dependence upon God in order to choose good and evil for themselves.

Genesis speaks of pain and suffering and hardship entering human life as a result of that first rebellion. God tells the woman that she will suffer pain in childbirth; he tells the man that the ground will be cursed and that work will be a burden. The biblical language encompasses the loss of all the blessings and wholeness God had intended for his creation. Disorder entered into the human condition—a disorder caused not by God but by man's refusal to obey God.

Sin and Sickness Today

I believe it is correct to say that even today all sickness, all disease, all human affliction and deterioration, is connected in some way to sin. That does *not* mean that every sick person is suffering for having done something wrong. We will not always see a direct connection on the personal level. But sometimes we can see a clear link between behavior and sickness, and those cases help us understand how affliction can come from our own sin.

Most obvious today is the appearance and rapid spread of very serious diseases through sexual promiscuity. Twenty years ago the media in this country began to speak of a sexual revolution. Various experts told us to throw off the "repressive" morality taught by our Judeo-Christian heritage and indulge ourselves in any kind of sexual behavior we desired. Thousands of people, especially our young people, heeded the call. Sex outside of marriage, homosexuality, casual sex, pornography—all were accepted and encouraged by the "new morality."

Yet there was nothing new in this: just the same rebellion against God and against God's laws. Everything we have seen in the sexual revolution was described long ago in St. Paul's letter to the Romans:

> The wrath of God is being revealed from heaven against the irreligious and perverse spirit of men who, in this perversity of theirs, hinder the truth.... They certainly had knowledge of God, yet they did not glorify him as God or give him thanks; they stultified themselves through speculating to no purpose, and their senseless hearts were darkened. ... In consequence, God delivered them up in their lusts to unclean practices; they engaged in the mutual degradation of their bodies, these men who exchanged the truth of God for a lie and worshiped and served the creature rather than the Creator—blessed be he forever, amen! (Rom 1:18, 21, 24-25)

Now, after twenty years of sexual revolution, our society is discovering the consequences of rejecting God's moral law. An epidemic of incurable, sometimes deadly diseases is occurring among thousands of people due to sexual contact. Doctors fear that the most serious of these new diseases, AIDS, may eventually become one of the nation's leading causes of death.

Now, I am not saying that God went out and created these horrible diseases in order to punish people for their sins. It would be more correct to say that sin creates its own punishment. When we violate the natural laws, when we fail to obey what God has revealed, we open ourselves up to a host of evils. We have removed ourselves from God's protection, and consequently we become far more vulnerable to all attacks of affliction, sickness, and unhappiness.

Of course, it is not just venereal diseases that show the connection between sin and sickness. Modern medical science has found many ways in which sickness is linked to a disordered life-style. We don't hear much these days about the sin of gluttony—which is not simply overeating but a selfish absorption in pleasing our tastes. But how many people are literally dying of heart disease and cancers caused by a gluttonous indulgence in foods and habits that they know are unhealthy?

Or consider the link between sickness and the emotions. Bitterness, hatred, resentment, jealousy, impatience, anger—these feelings can literally poison us if we don't resolve them, repent of them, forgive the other people involved, and replace those feelings with the peace that comes through Jesus Christ.

Bitterness Can Kill

Some years ago a woman came to me for prayers for healing. She was suffering from a host of afflictions, including migraine headaches, heart palpitations, and ulcers. As I started to pray with her, I felt an inner prompting—which I believe is one way God speaks to us—to ask whether something else lay behind her illnesses.

"Is there anything else going on in your life that I should know?" I asked.

She was quite offended and told me in so many words to mind my own business. Clearly, she wanted me just to say a few words of prayer and not get too personal. But I didn't have much choice.

"Look," I told her, "I don't put a price on praying with people. But if you want me to help you, you've got to be honest with me. Isn't there something else troubling you that you're not telling me?"

With that she started to cry, and the whole story came spilling out. Five years before, a Catholic priest had mistakenly accused her of wrongdoing. She lost her job as a consequence, and with the black mark on her record, she was unable to find another.

Naturally, she was angry at the injustice she had suffered, and the anger in itself was not wrong. But she had allowed the anger to fester and grow into a resentment that was literally eating her up. When the Lord tells us to "forgive those who have trespassed against us," he means those who have hurt us—not those who always have something nice to say. Bitterness or hatred that grows from a just cause can be every bit as deadly as that which starts out wrong.

I led the woman through a prayer of forgiveness, unloading all the pain and resentment she had carried with her for five years. She made her confession to me and received absolution. I heard from her later that she had finally been able to go speak to the priest who had hurt her and explain her side of the whole story. He was so touched that he retracted all his charges and helped her get a new job, even better than the old one.

Above all, every single symptom of her sickness had disappeared. The headaches, the heart problems, the ulcers—all had vanished. Her sickness had been the physical manifestation of resentment and unforgiveness. Once her bitterness was resolved, her health returned.

Don't Blameless People Get Sick?

I have seen many such cases where sickness was clearly linked to some sinful behavior or bitterness. Yet many other times the explanation has not been so easy. People who live exemplary Christian lives still get sick. Men and women of real sanctity, who give themselves in loving service to God and others, still suffer painful illness and affliction. Infants are born with genetic diseases and birth defects that obviously have nothing to do with their behavior or their parents'.

How can I link sickness to sin when so many people suffer blamelessly?

The fact of innocent suffering has troubled theologians and philosophers of every age. I do not pretend to understand all the mysteries of God's will in this matter, but I do believe the essential truth remains: Sickness and affliction come not from God but from human sin and rebellion.

Even if we ourselves strive to remain faithful, we suffer the effects of living in a world where sin is rampant. We see this very directly when we are hurt by someone else's spitefulness. We see it in the sufferings caused by war and economic upheaval and crime—all manifestations of sin in our world. We see it in our own inner struggles with temptation and sin.

The fact is, we live in a world where things do not happen according to God's original plan. Just as personal sin leaves an individual more vulnerable to all kinds of affliction, so too the sins of the human race have left all human beings weakened and vulnerable. This is part of what we mean by the term "original sin." From the point of conception, before we have any ability to commit a personal sin, we are affected by the fact that we belong to a sinful humanity.

Sickness is one consequence of that general human sinfulness. It is possible to suffer a sickness caused by another person's sin, even when we have had no part in it. Among the victims of the dreaded new venereal diseases are many people innocent of any sexual immorality, who were infected by an unfaithful spouse or a contaminated blood transfusion. We can take an even broader view: The greatest single cause of sickness throughout the world is poverty, which is ultimately caused by the sin of human selfishness.

Even where we cannot draw any direct link to some sinful behavior—as in the case of genetic diseases—sickness reflects the weakness and vulnerability and disorder that entered human life because of sin.

No, God is not to blame for sickness. The responsibility lies squarely on our own doorstep.

Sickness, Sin and Salvation

Wouldn't it be depressing if we had to stop right there, if Scripture only revealed that we ourselves bear the blame for the world's afflictions and suffering—and there was nothing we could do about it?

Thanks be to God, we don't stop there. Because God was not content to let sin destroy his creation and his original plan. God decided to save us from sin and from all the consequences of sin—including sickness.

The story Genesis tells of our first parents' sin also contains the first promise that God would one day deal with sin. God vows to put enmity between the serpent—Satan—and the offspring of the woman. One day the woman's offspring will crush the serpent's head (see Gn 3:15).

In the history of the Jewish people—the people God chose and made his own—the promise of God's salvation became more clearly understood. The Jewish prophets spoke of the day when death and pain would be no more, when the blind would see and cripples walk and the deaf hear (see Is 25:8; 35:3-10).

But how would God's promised salvation come about?

Obviously, God could have simply stepped in to change the human personality so that we would no longer be able to sin. Sin would be eradicated from human life, and all the suffering and pain caused by sin would vanish too. But if God had done that, we would be a great deal less than the human beings he originally created. We would no longer have a true will or choice of our own. We would not be able to love God as he intended, because we would have no ability *not* to love God.

God had a very different plan for our salvation. He did not just sweep away sin and all its effects, because he wanted to leave us free to choose. But he formed a plan that would turn the very consequences of sin—

sickness and pain and death—into the means of our salvation.

Perhaps the best way to explain God's plan to deal with the suffering caused by sin is to tell the story of a blind man who lived a long time ago.

THREE

God's Plan

NO ONE EVEN GLANCED AT THE BLIND MAN as he tapped his way down the crowded street. He was a familiar sight in this part of Jerusalem—one of the hundreds of beggars who squatted in the dirt at the busiest street corners, wheedling coins from the pilgrims on their way to the temple to pray. The local people usually ignored them.

Of course they all knew this one. He'd been born right here in the neighborhood. A punishment for sin, they'd all agreed, when word got out that his mother had given birth to a blind baby. The family had always seemed respectable enough, but the father must have done something terrible once that nobody knew about. Or maybe it was the mother—or both of them, for that matter.

Well, whatever they'd done, they were paying for it now. For some twenty years the family with the blind child had been pointed out throughout the neighborhood as proof that your sins will catch up with you.

The young man reached his chosen spot just as unfamiliar voices were drawing near. Not from Jerusalem, he wagered—those were Galilean accents.

Quite a little crowd of them too. Must be pilgrims still in town from the recent festival.

"Help a poor blind man!" he called. "Alms for a poor sinner who was born blind!"

Ah, they'd stopped.

"Brothers, won't you help a poor son of Abraham who was born blind?" he entreated, with his best beggar's whine. One of them pressed a coin into his hand. A lousy drachma, he grumbled to himself as he called, "Oh, bless you! Bless you for your mercy!" to what should have been their departing backs. People who gave him money always rushed off—before the family sin could rub off on them, he supposed.

But the little band of Galileans was not moving on.

"Teacher," he heard one of them ask another, "why was this man born blind? Was it to punish his sins or his parents' sins?"

Just my luck, the blind man thought bitterly. Another wandering rabbi with his disciples. Now I can be their lesson for the day: See how God punishes the sinner! For once I wish someone would explain to *me* what sin a baby could have committed before he was even born. Or what my poor parents ever did wrong.

Yet the rabbi's answer surprised him.

"Neither," he said. "It was no sin, either of this man or of his parents. Rather, it was to let God's work show forth in him. We must do the deeds of him who sent me while it is day. The night comes on when no man can work. While I am in the world, I am the light of the world."

I've heard some strange rabbis, thought the blind man, but this one . . . ! I wonder if it's that fellow I've heard talk about, the one they call Jesus.

With a start, he realized that the rabbi was standing right in front of him now. The man was spitting on the ground, then rubbing something on his eyes—some kind of mud.

"Go," the rabbi told him. "Wash in the pool of Siloam."

The one thing the blind man could never quite explain later was why he obeyed the stranger without a question. All he knew was that he found himself at the pool of Siloam a few minutes later, washing the mud from his eyes. As he washed, his eyes began burning. Something seemed to be flooding into his head, something that moved and dazzled and filled him with sensations he had never known.

"What's going on there?" a voice behind him yelled. "Is that beggar having a fit?"

The blind man whirled around, and all the strange somethings whirled too. Then it hit him: This is light. *Light!* I can see!

He was shouting now. *"I can see!"*

Jesus: God's Answer to Sickness

The story of Jesus' encounter with the man born blind speaks to many questions discussed in the last chapter: Are sin and sickness connected? Why do innocent people suffer physical afflictions? How could birth defects and genetic illnesses be linked to sin? And most importantly; What does God want to do about sickness?

In Jesus God gave his answer to our questions. He had already revealed to his chosen people, the people of Israel, that sickness and affliction were not his plan for us but a result of human rebellion and sin. Yet God was not interested in simply fixing the blame for our suffering—whether on our own sins or someone else's sin or the general sinfulness of humanity. His greatest desire was to set us free from the consequences of sin and restore the harmony of his creation.

And so God sent his own Son into the world as one of us, to bear the pain and suffering that resulted from human sin. The blameless one suffered the penalty of sin, so that we who were guilty could be set free.

> It was our infirmities that he bore,
> our sufferings that he endured,
> While we thought of him as stricken,
> as one smitten by God and afflicted.
> But he was pierced for our offenses,
> crushed for our sins;
> Upon him was the chastisement that makes us whole,
> by his stripes we were healed.
> (Is 53:4-5)

By his suffering, death, and resurrection, Jesus has restored the covenant relationship with God that man destroyed through rebellion. Through Jesus, and through Jesus alone, God now offers to restore to us the harmony, the order, the purity, that he intended from the beginning. He offers victory over sin—our own sins and the sins of our world. He offers victory over all the pain and evil that sin introduced into human life.

This is why healings—like the healing of the man born blind—occupied so much of Jesus' ministry on earth. Jesus worked miracles, not to show off his power, but to reveal his purpose in coming into the world. His power over sickness was only a sign of his far greater power over sin. "Which is less trouble to say," he once asked the scribes who criticized him, " 'Your sins are forgiven' or 'Stand up and walk?' " (Mt 9:5).

In healing the sick Jesus was pushing back the darkness, undoing the effects of sin, freeing people from bondage to the evil one. He was restoring God's reign in human life—the harmony that God had intended for us from the beginning. So it was that when John the Baptist sent his disciples to ask whether Jesus was the promised Messiah, Jesus answered:

"Go and report to John what you have seen and heard. The blind recover their sight, cripples walk, lepers are cured, the deaf hear, dead men are raised to life, and the poor have the good news preached to them" (Lk 7:22).

Healing was the great sign given by Jesus to show that God's salvation had arrived.

God's Reign in Our Lives

When we now enter into a covenant relationship with Jesus Christ, we also enter into his victory over sin and sickness and death.

Obviously that does not mean that Christians never become sick or never die. We are still living in a world where sin is rampant; we still must struggle against our own sinfulness and all its consequences. The full victory lies in the future, when Jesus Christ returns to reign over a new heaven and a new earth. Then, as the book of Revelation promises, "He shall dwell with them, and they shall be his people and he shall be their God who is always with them. He shall wipe every tear from their eyes, and there shall be no more death or mourning, crying out or pain, for the former world has passed away" (Rv 21:3-4).

Yet even now, while we await the fulfillment of these promises, Jesus does change our experience of sickness and suffering. We can be healed and have victory over sickness as we submit our lives more fully to the reign of God.

I know many people who will testify that as they surrendered their lives more fully to Jesus, they experienced greater physical health and strength. One is my good friend Margaret Cavnar of Dallas, Texas. Margaret's husband Bob is the man who encouraged me to extend my preaching ministry through television; he now produces my weekly program, *The Glory of God.*

At one point a few years ago, before we found other facilities, Bob and Margaret's home served as the offices for our television ministry—with six or seven people working there every day. I also stayed at the house whenever I came to Dallas to work on the program, and a young couple with a newborn baby were living there too. Bob and Margaret usually had a few other houseguests as well, and they hosted a dozen meetings every week to boot.

I often wondered where Margaret found the stamina to keep up with such a household. Then one day I heard her story.

"There was a time when this kind of life would have killed me," Margaret explained. "I was practically a physical wreck."

I learned that Margaret had actually suffered years of ill health: severe anemia, chronic back pain from an injury, multiple allergies. In 1967 she nearly died following a routine surgery, because her blood vessels were so weak they could not stop hemorrhaging. In 1970 Margaret was seeing three doctors regularly and had a kitchen cabinet filled with prescriptions.

Then came an event that turned the Cavnars' whole life upside down. On a visit to Ann Arbor, Michigan, where two of their children had become part of a charismatic renewal community, Bob and Margaret experienced the outpouring of the Holy Spirit that we call being "baptized in the Spirit." They returned to Dallas on fire with a renewed faith in the Lord.

One morning, not long afterward, Margaret came out to the kitchen to collect all the pills for her morning medication. In the evening she would take more pills, and then there were the allergy shots that Bob gave her each day.

This morning, though, as Margaret looked down at her handful of pills and capsules, she asked herself, "What am I taking these for? They haven't made me feel any better. Surely the Lord can take better care of me than this." On the spot, to the horror of the cleaning woman who was standing nearby, Margaret cleared out all her medicines and threw every bottle in the trash.

I want to stress here that I do *not* advocate Christians throwing their medicines away. Neither does Margaret Cavnar, for that matter. The medical profession is an important part of the total healing ministry, and we should respect its help. Yet many doctors will tell you that people often come to them with complaints they cannot heal, because the real problem is more spiritual than physical.

The realization that hit Margaret on that morning in her kitchen was not that medicine is useless but that she had never really turned her health over to the Lord. She wanted to make a completely fresh start in how she sought health. None of her problems were life-threatening, and the worst that could result from stopping her medicines was increased discomfort from her back pain and allergy symptoms.

Instead her health blossomed. "I had never felt so well in my life," she says. "No back pain or other problems, and I had more energy than ever before. For at least three years I never even had a cold."

After three or four years of what she calls "super-natural health," Margaret experienced a return of the occasional health problems most of us suffer, including some serious flare-ups of her back trouble. She goes to the doctor when necessary and takes any prescribed medication. She has also learned to take a more active role in protecting her health through proper exercise and nutrition. Yet today, after twenty years, her health remains far stronger than it was for the twenty years before she learned that the Lord would be her healer.

Fighting Affliction

Margaret told me that one of the most important lessons she has learned about health is to fight for it.

"I believe that God doesn't want me to be sick," she explains. "So when I start to feel any symptom of sickness, I fight it. I fight with prayer and by keeping an attitude of faith that God will keep me well. I'll fight with medical means too, if necessary. But many times when I start out fighting on the spiritual level, my symptoms stop without ever developing into anything serious."

To some people this attitude of fighting sickness may seem out of step with Catholic spiritual tradition, which has always emphasized the redemptive value of suffering. Many of us were taught to accept sickness and pain as God's will. We were given the example of great saints who suffered long, painful illnesses joyfully, accepting them as a share in the suffering of Jesus.

In a later chapter I will discuss how God can use suffering in our lives—for suffering can indeed be a source of real spiritual strength. But the fact that God can turn suffering to good does not mean that he wants to inflict sickness and pain on us. Everything we have considered about the origin of sickness, everything we see concerning healing in Jesus' ministry, shows that God wants us to fight affliction—in our own lives and in the lives of all around us.

As disciples of Jesus, we are actually commanded to fight sickness. Jesus sent his disciples to minister in the world with "authority to expel unclean spirits and to cure sickness and disease of every kind"(Mt 10:1). "Make this announcement," he told them: " 'The reign of God is at hand!' Cure the sick, raise the dead, heal the leprous, expel demons" (Mt 10:7-8).

Jesus initiated the reign of God, but he left it to us, his disciples, to continue extending God's reign on the earth. It is now our task to continue his work of pushing back the power of darkness. He has given us power, in the gift of his Holy Spirit, to wage his battle against every form of affliction.

We see this clearly in the life of the apostolic church, as recorded in the Acts of the Apostles. "Many wonders and signs were performed by the apostles" (Acts 2:43), and foremost among them were healings. "The people carried the sick into the streets and laid them on cots and mattresses, so that when Peter passed by at least his shadow might fall on one or another of them. Crowds from the towns around Jerusalem would gather, too, bringing their sick and those who were troubled by unclean spirits, all of whom were cured" (Acts 5:15-16).

Healing was an integral part of the good news the apostles proclaimed. Acts tells of Peter and John meeting a crippled beggar at the temple gate and telling him, "I have neither silver nor gold, but what I have I give you! In the name of Jesus Christ, the Nazorean, walk!" (Acts 3:6). And "immediately the beggar's feet and ankles became strong; he jumped up, stood for a moment, then began to walk around" (Acts 3:7-8). To the crowd attracted by this miracle, Peter proclaimed: "It is [Jesus'] name, and trust in this name, that has strengthened the limbs of this man whom you see and know well. Such faith has given him perfect health, as all of you can observe" (Acts 3:16).

The letter of James, which reflects a slightly later period in the church's life, shows that healing remained part of the ministry of the presbyters, the ordained servant-leaders of the early Christian community. "Is there anyone sick among you?" asks James. "He should ask for the presbyters of the church. They in turn are to pray over him, anointing him with oil in the Name [of the Lord]. This prayer uttered in faith will reclaim the one who is ill, and the Lord will restore him to health" (Jas 5:14-15).

Proclaiming Christ's Victory

Through the nineteen hundred years since the time of the apostles, the fight against sickness and suffering has remained an essential part of the church's ministry. The official prayers and sacraments of the church are filled with the expectation that God will heal our afflictions. The history of renewal movements within the church and the lives of the saints contain numerous stories of healing, as Jesus' followers have proclaimed his victory over affliction.

God's people have fought suffering and sickness through other means as well: through loving care for the sick, through medical discoveries, through any means that would relieve the suffering of the afflicted. We often fail to realize how much the modern attitude of compassion and care for the sick owes to our Christian heritage. In many earlier cultures the sick were not cared for but were abandoned or killed.

Even today, when Christian missionaries go out to other areas of the world to proclaim the gospel, they go as ministers of healing—building hospitals and clinics, providing medical care for the poor, teaching people how to stay well.

The example of Jesus, of the apostolic church, and of God's people in every age since calls us to continue the fight against affliction in the name of our Lord. We too can share in Jesus' victory over sickness; we too can proclaim that victory to the world. Our basic stance concerning sickness should always be to ask for healing, to ask God to intervene, while doing all we can do ourselves to relieve and heal the sick.

God has given us many means, both spiritual and natural, to fight affliction and seek his healing. In the next chapter we will take a closer look at how to receive God's victory over sickness.

FOUR

Seeking Healing

I F WE BELIEVE THAT GOD WANTS TO HEAL US, what do we do about it? How do we seek his gift of healing?

There's really nothing complicated or mysterious about prayer for healing. Simply ask. You don't have to use just the right words, you don't have to work up a particular degree of faith, you don't have to find the most gifted healing minister. Simply go to your Father, ask for his help, and trust that he will be with you.

"Ask, and you will receive," Jesus told us. "Would one of you hand his son a stone when he asks for a loaf, or a poisonous snake when he asks for a fish? If you, with all your sins, know how to give your children what is good, how much more will your heavenly Father give good things to anyone who asks him!" (Mt 7:7-11).

I believe that from the moment we ask for healing—if not before—we can trust that God is helping us. Where we must learn more about healing is not so much in how to ask, but in how to respond. Are we open to the Lord's healing work? Are we actively pursuing all the means to healing he has given us?

We can take an example from ordinary medical wisdom. Suppose a heavy smoker goes to his doctor with early symptoms of emphysema. His doctor tells him to stop smoking, but the man keeps right on smoking. The emphysema grows worse and finally kills him.

Did that man die because the doctor refused to heal him? Of course not. The man died because he himself refused to throw away his cigarettes. He refused to respond to the doctor's care in a way that might have enabled him to regain his health.

In the same way, we can fail to recognize and respond to the ways God offers us healing. The Lord is at work to help us and deliver us from affliction. Yet he expects us to take our place in the fight. I call this active faith: We do not sit back passively and wait for God to send a miracle from the sky, but we move forward aggressively to fight for health and for healing, confident that God is fighting with us.

Our active response to God's healing work must encompass all three dimensions of our human nature: physical, psychological, and spiritual. Sometimes we need to take action against sickness on the physical level: stop smoking, lose weight, eat a balanced diet, get more exercise, get more sleep, take the right medication. Some times we need to take action on the psychological level: deal with stress and emotional conflicts that might be causing physical problems. And always we need to take action on the spiritual level, turning to the Lord in obedience and faith.

Turning to Jesus

The response of faith is always the starting point in our fight against affliction. If we want to open our lives to God's healing love, we must make sure we are in the right relationship with Jesus Christ. How can we call upon God as our Father if we are not joined to his Son? How can we receive salvation from affliction and death if we are cut off from the Savior?

All that I am saying about God's healing can make sense only in the context of a faith relationship with Jesus Christ. If we want to experience God's victory over sickness and affliction, either for ourselves or for those we love, we must enter into a relationship with Jesus Christ. The awesome mystery of suffering and sickness and death can only be embraced if I have embraced the crucified and risen Lord.

Whenever I minister to someone in need of healing, my first concern is always to lead the person into a closer relationship with Jesus Christ. Evangelism and healing go hand in hand: At the heart of every prayer for healing is a prayer of surrender to Jesus as the Lord and Savior of our lives. Even those of us who have committed our lives to Jesus are always in need of a deeper conversion as we realize the ways we have not yet fully accepted his Lordship over us.

One way to express the fact that God's healing comes to us through our relationship with Jesus is that we always pray for healing in the name of Jesus. He himself has promised: ". . . whatever you ask in my name I will do, so as to glorify the Father in the Son" (Jn 14:13). When Peter and John healed the cripple at the Temple gates, it was with the words: "In the name of Jesus Christ, the Nazorean, walk!" (Acts 3:6). They told the crowd, "It is his name, and trust in this name, that has strengthened the limbs of this man whom you see and know well" (Acts 3:16).

To pray for healing in the name of Jesus means much

more than to use his name mechanically, as if it were some kind of magic word. In ancient times, when the Scriptures were written, to know someone's name meant to know the person himself. Knowledge of a person's name gave you a claim on that person; it established a relationship between you.

To pray in Jesus' name, then, means that our prayer is rooted in a personal relationship with him. It means to have trust in Jesus. It means to have faith in Jesus. It means to be living under the Lordship of Jesus, following his teaching day after day. It means to be joined personally to Jesus, to know him as brother, as friend, and as Savior. It is the power that comes from the person of Jesus that brings healing into our lives.

Repentance

As we enter into a new relationship with Jesus, we must begin to deal with any sin in our lives. When Jesus promises to do whatever we ask in his name, he adds only one condition: "If you love me and obey the commands I give you ..." (Jn 14:15). Just a few verses later, the words are recorded again: "He who obeys the commandments he has from me is the man who loves me" (Jn 14:21). Love for Jesus and obedience to his commandments go hand in hand.

Of course, we all know ways we do not obey Jesus' commandments—ways we fail in our love for the Lord and for the other people around us. Even after we have committed our lives to the Lord and are seeking to follow him faithfully, we still fail. That is why repentance is not a one-time event when we first commit our lives to the Lord, but an ongoing process. Every day we must acknowledge the ways we have failed to love the Lord and obey his commandments. Every day we must decide again to follow Jesus Christ.

Once we recognize the link between sin and sickness, we can see why repentance is so important to healing. Unrepented sin in our lives can block God's healing work on two levels. In some cases unrepented sin may lie at the very root of our physical sickness; until we deal with the sin, we cannot deal with sickness. In other cases, where the sickness itself is not directly related to sin, unrepented sin still creates an obstacle between us and the Lord. We cannot pray in the name of Jesus if at the same time we are cutting ourselves off from Jesus by refusing to turn away from sin.

I encounter many, many people who experience a direct link between repentance and healing. One man told me how he had been caught up in an almost compulsive fascination with pornography. He knew pornography was wrong, but he could not keep away from it.

Meanwhile, he was suffering spells of extreme dizziness that kept growing more severe and frightening. One day, it occurred to him that perhaps these episodes were related to his sinful obsession with pornography. He destroyed his collection of pornographic materials, then went to confession and asked the Lord's forgiveness. From that time on, all of the disturbing physical symptoms ceased.

Just as unrepented sin can lead to sickness, repentance can indeed be good medicine.

Laying on of Hands

Healing takes place through our relationship with Jesus—through faith, conversion, and repentance.

Yet while Jesus can act in our lives directly, he will most often touch us through our brothers and sisters in the body of Christ. After all, the Son of God has shown by his own Incarnation that he wants to work through our humanity—our very flesh and blood. That is why, even as we ask the Lord directly for healing, we also turn to each other as ministers of his healing power.

One of the greatest symbols by which we minister the Lord's healing to each other is to pray with laying on of hands. This is a very simple gesture: As I pray, I place my hands on the person's head or—with localized problems like back pain or a tumor—directly on the afflicted area.

The laying on of hands is a gesture with deep roots in our Judeo-Christian heritage. In the Old Testament, it was used as a gesture of blessing (Gn 48:12-16) and of consecration (Lv 1:4). In the New Testament, the laying on of hands is a gesture of healing (Mk 6:5) and of the gift of the Holy Spirit (Acts 19:6).

The Catholic church considers the laying on of hands to be a sacramental—that is, a gesture that invokes the prayers of the whole church. Since the Second Vatican Council, the use of this gesture has been revived in the administration of all of the sacraments. But the laying on of hands can also be used by both priests and lay people in prayers apart from the sacraments.

When I am asked why I use the laying on of hands so much in praying with people, I point out that at every mass we see the priest place his hands over the gifts of bread and wine on the altar, asking the Holy Spirit to come upon them and transform them into the Body and Blood of Jesus. Why should it then be unusual for us to see hands extended over a person, as we ask the Holy Spirit to fill and transform that person?

Such a laying on of hands has a three-dimensional meaning, corresponding to the three dimensions of the human person. Spiritually, the gesture is a way of channeling the power of the Holy Spirit. Anytime the church calls forth the Spirit—at Baptism, at Confirmation, at Holy Orders—there is a laying on of hands. It expresses our desire to have Jesus touch a person and fill that person with his Holy Spirit. One of our great privileges as Christians is to serve as channels by which the Spirit can touch others.

On the psychological level, the laying on of hands expresses a sense of closeness and concern. It expresses our human love, which is itself a healing force. If we wish to minister healing to others, we cannot be indifferent or detached from their needs. The laying on of hands speaks of our solidarity with them, our love for them, our caring.

Finally, on the physical level, the touch of our hands is a way of comforting a person in sickness or pain, in the same way as a hug or an embrace. Some studies even suggest that physical touch communicates a healing energy, so that hospital patients recover faster when the nurses make a point of simple, caring gestures of touch.

The laying on of hands is much more than a ritual gesture, then. It truly communicates love, concern, and the power of the Holy Spirit. It says, "I care. I care about your suffering. I care that you receive healing." Prayer with the laying on of hands is one way we can minister the Lord's healing love to others.

Deliverance

In the Gospels, Jesus' miracles of healing are often linked with the expulsion of evil spirits. "... all who had people sick with a variety of diseases took them to him," recounts the Gospel of Luke, "and he laid hands on each of them and cured them. Demons departed from many, crying out as they did so, 'You are the Son of God!'" (Lk 4:40-41).

Some modern biblical scholars have suggested that Gospel passages like this simply reflect some primitive beliefs about evil spirits. Yet I believe the Gospel actually has a very important truth to teach us. The Catholic church has always warned of the reality of evil spirits, who war against God's people. It was through the malice of Satan that sin first entered our world, and Satan and his evil spirits continue to seek our destruction. "Stay sober and alert," warns the first letter of Peter. "Your opponent the devil is prowling like a roaring lion looking for someone to devour" (1 Pt 5:8).

Satan's attacks upon us generally take the form of temptations to sin and other spiritual assaults. Yet as we see in the Gospels, Satan can sometimes attack us through physical problems and afflictions. Satan may simply try to undermine our confidence in the Lord when we are sick, by playing on our fears or our feelings of discouragement or bitterness. In some cases, sickness might even be directly caused by an attack of the evil one.

Unfortunately, Christians often overreact to the suggestion of demonic assault. I believe we need to recognize the reality of Satan's work, but not with any exaggerated fear or fascination. The Lord offers us all the protection and strength we need to withstand spiritual attacks. As Paul says, "... draw your strength from the Lord and his mighty power. Put on the armor of God so that you may be able to stand firm against the tactics of the devil. ... In all circumstances hold faith up before you as your shield; it will help you extinguish the fiery darts of the evil one. Take the helmet of salvation and the sword of the Spirit, the word of God" (Eph 6:10-17).

Whenever I am ministering to someone in need of healing, I always ask the Lord for discernment about whether any demonic influence might be involved. If I feel that perhaps there is, I always bring it up with the person: "Have you ever felt that some spiritual power is playing a part in this illness?" If the person feels that might be true, then together we will pray for the Lord's protection against any spiritual assault. I often use a prayer that was once part of the rite for the Sacrament of the Sick:

> May any power that the devil has over you be utterly destroyed, as I place my hands upon you and call upon the help of the glorious and holy Mother of God, the Virgin Mary, and of her illustrious spouse, Joseph, and of all the holy Angels, Archangels, patriarchs, prophets, apostles, martyrs, confessors, virgins, and all the saints.

In my own devotional life, I have found great value in many of the sacramentals and traditional prayers of the church that ask for God's protection against the power of the evil one. The sign of the cross, holy water, blessed salt, the rosary—these are all ways to call upon the Lord for protection and spiritual strength. One prayer that has become very important to me is the traditional Litany of the Precious Blood, which invokes the power of the Blood of Jesus to cleanse us and protect us.

Persistent Faith

In one of his most down-to-earth parables, Jesus spoke to his disciples about not giving up when prayers seem to go unanswered:

> "Once there was a judge in a certain city who respected neither God nor man. A widow in that city kept coming to him saying, 'Give me my rights against my opponent.' For a time he refused, but finally he thought, 'I care little for God or man, but this widow is wearing me out. I am going to settle in her favor or she will end by doing me violence.'" The Lord said, "Listen to what the corrupt judge has to say. Will not God then do justice to his chosen who call out to him day and night? Will he delay long over them, do you suppose? I tell you, he will give them swift justice." (Lk 18:2-8)

There is something humorous in the picture of us wearing out God as the widow wore out the judge. But in drawing this humorous picture, the Lord offers us an important truth. It is only too easy to get discouraged when prayers for healing do not produce an immediate change in our physical condition. We always need the reminder that we must persist day by day in turning to the Lord with faith.

Some Christians approach persistent prayer almost as if they really did have to wear down God's resistance and force him to heal them. I believe they are missing the real point of the Lord's parable. God is not a corrupt judge who has to be pressured into concern for us; he is our loving Father, who always cares for us and our needs.

To persist in faith for healing simply means that we continue trusting in our Father's love. We trust that he knows our sickness and suffering, that he wants to set us free, that he will meet every one of our needs. We trust that he will deal with our illness in the way that brings us the greatest good.

It is in living out our trust in the Lord, day after day, that we need persistence. Often at the start of a period of sickness or affliction, we find it easy to be strong in faith. But as weeks and months and years go by, the struggle with discouragement grows tougher. That is why daily prayer is so important to the process of healing. We turn to the Lord each day in petition and supplication—not because he needs a reminder of our needs but because we ourselves need the daily reminder of his loving concern.

The Scriptures place great emphasis on living one day at a time. "Let tomorrow take care of itself," Jesus said. "Today has troubles enough of its own" (Mt 6:34). And he taught his disciples to pray, "Give us this day our daily bread."

I believe that in the same way, we must approach healing one day at a time. Each day we ask the Lord for health and strength and courage, and each day the Lord will give us whatever we need to meet the demands of that day. If he does not take away our physical problems that day, we can be sure that he will give us the spiritual energy and strength to cope with suffering. From a great deal of experience in ministering to the sick and dying, I know that even those who are terminally ill will receive what they need from the Lord to face their end.

The most important step we can take to pursue healing is to turn to the Lord daily with persistent, heartfelt prayer. "Present your needs to God in every form of prayer and in petitions full of gratitude," the Scripture urges us (Phil 4:6). I am often struck by the way people in a hospital look forward to their doctor's daily visit. They eagerly await the slightest word of encouragement or hope. How much more eagerly should we be looking to the Divine Physician? How much more important is it that we take the time each day to turn to him in prayer?

What about Medicine?

People sometimes ask me if I believe that Christians should rely only on prayer for healing, or if I also believe in using medical means. My answer is that I believe in the full healing ministry as revealed to us in Scripture. Medicine, doctors, hospitals, and research are as much a part of the Christian healing ministry as prayer and repentance and faith. In all these efforts, the scientific no less than the spiritual, it is God who acts to relieve suffering and free us from affliction.

The Old Testament Book of Sirach speaks of medicine and doctors as part of God's healing activity. "Hold the physician in honor," says Sirach, "for he is essential to you, / and God it was who established his profession. / From God the doctor has his wisdom.... / God makes the earth yield healing herbs. . . . / He endows men with the knowledge / to glory in his mighty works, / Through which the doctor eases pain / and the druggist prepares his medicines" (Sir 38:1-7).

Medicine is truly God's gift to us, and if we are healed through medical means we should thank and praise God as heartily as if we had been miraculously cured. As Christians who believe in God's healing, we can fully support all the research efforts to find medical cures for diseases. We can praise God for all the progress modern medicine has made in the fight against sickness.

We should also be praying for the doctors and nurses and medical researchers themselves. How wonderful it would be if all our scientists and doctors were consciously seeking God's wisdom and praying for him to act through their efforts.

One of the most exciting developments I have seen in the healing ministry has occurred as Christian doctors begin combining their medical wisdom with prayer for their patients. A few years ago at a conference in New Orleans, Louisiana, I met Dr. Bill Mitchell, a local Catholic physician who has added prayer to his black bag. Dr. Mitchell recounted some of the truly remarkable healings he has witnessed as he calls more directly on God's wisdom and intervention in his medical practice.

On one occasion, Dr. Mitchell happened to be in a hospital emergency room when a patient suffered a cardiac arrest. The medical team immediately went to work trying to revive the woman. Dr. Mitchell quietly worked his way to the edge of the action, where he could just touch the woman's ankle, and began to pray.

The emergency room doctor spotted him.

"Bill, quick," he said. "Would you take over the heart massage?" Dr. Mitchell was suddenly thrust into the center of the feverishly-working team. All of the woman's vital signs had stopped. He kept praying.

At that moment, Dr. Mitchell felt an inner prompting that he believed was from God:

"Bind a spirit of affliction and cast it out of her!"

Without stopping to worry what the other doctor would think, Dr. Mitchell commanded aloud with the very first push of the massage, "In the name of Jesus, I bind a spirit of affliction and command you to leave her!"

Instantly, the woman's heart began beating.

"Now call on my Spirit of life to fill her," that inner voice of the Lord told him.

"Lord God, fill this woman with your Holy Spirit of Life," Dr. Mitchell prayed aloud. The woman's eyes popped open, and she sat up.

Dr. Mitchell has had many equally remarkable experiences. "Whenever I am seeing a patient," he says, "I'm praying to myself the whole time, asking the Lord to show me what is really going on with this person. So many times, I will receive an insight that could never have come from my own knowledge."

How wonderful it would be if all our scientists and doctors were consciously seeking God's wisdom and help in this way. As great as our modern medical science is, it could only be greater for being filled with more of the Lord's power.

Putting It All Together

That may be the most important lesson of this chapter: All of the healing ministries fit together. It is not a question of prayer *or* medicine, repentance *or* deliverance, the hospital *or* the church. God's healing power flows through many channels at once; he can be working at the same time on the physical level through medical means and on the emotional level though psychological means and on the spiritual level through prayer for healing and deliverance.

The Book of Sirach, which teaches us so much about the gift of medical science, outlines what I consider the ideal pattern of response to illness—a response open to every avenue of God's healing:

> My son, when you are ill, delay not,
> but pray to God, who will heal you:
> Flee wickedness, let your hands be just,
> cleanse your heart of every sin;
> Offer your sweet-smelling oblation and petition,
> a rich offering according to your means.
> Then give the doctor his place
> lest he leave; for you need him too.
> There are times that give him an advantage,
> and he too beseeches God
> That his diagnosis may be correct
> and his treatment bring about a cure. (Sir 38:9-14)

Here we see a pattern that fits with all the avenues of healing we have just discussed. Our very first response to illness is to turn to God immediately, unhesitatingly. "Delay not," Sirach tells us, and how much more we who know Jesus can appreciate his urgency.

Then, knowing that sickness can be a consequence of sin, we strike at the root of our affliction by dealing with any sin in our lives. "Flee wickedness," says Sirach: Break any pattern of sinful behavior. "Let your hands be just": Seek reconciliation with any you have mistreated or offended. "Cleanse your heart of sin": Turn to God in repentance and sorrow to receive his forgiveness.

Sirach speaks next of the Old Testament practice of offering sacrifice—"sweet-smelling oblation and petition"—as a means of intercession before God. As we will see in the next chapter, we can take part in the greatest of all sacrifices—Jesus' own offering of his life upon the cross.

And then, in conjunction with our prayer and repentance and on-going conversion, we turn also to our doctors and allow God to work through them. "Then give the doctor his place lest he leave, for you need him too." We do not turn to medicine apart from Jesus; neither do we neglect the human healing ministries God has blessed. A full, complete understanding of God's healing work will encompass both the wonders of medicine and the wonder of his mercy and forgiveness and love.

FIVE

Sacraments

I F YOU WANT TO KNOW WHAT A CHURCH BELIEVES, study what it prays.

That saying expresses a basic principle for many theological studies. The official prayers and liturgy of church provide the best guide to what that church really believes and teaches. That is why any change in the official prayers produces such an uproar—as the Catholic church discovered after the liturgical reforms of Vatican II. When you change the way people pray, you seem to threaten their basic beliefs as well.

If we want to know what the Catholic church believes about healing, then, we need to study what it prays. And when we study the prayers and sacraments of the Catholic church, we find a profound expression of faith in God's power to heal us. All the connections made in the last chapter—between healing and conversion, healing and repentance, healing and deliverance—can be found right in the liturgy of the Catholic church. The most powerful healing services around are celebrated every day in your local Catholic parish.

Sadly, many of the Catholics who take part in these celebrations—including many of the priests who lead them—come with no real expectation for healing or personal change. The renewal of the charismatic healing ministry has begun to change that situation, and some parishes now celebrate the sacraments with real faith in their healing power. Yet the fact that our own parish may need further renewal and change should not blind us to the great riches of the liturgy and sacraments themselves.

What Is a Sacrament?

To appreciate the power of the church's official prayers and sacraments, we need to understand the full spiritual reality they contain. Have you ever wished you could walk up to Jesus himself, as the people in the Gospels did, to ask him to heal you? That is exactly what happens in the sacraments. The sacraments are not just human rituals and ceremonies. They are the actions of Jesus himself, ministering to us through his body on earth, the church.

Jesus devoted much of his earthly ministry to forming a group of men who would call his followers together in a community, a people. He gave them authority to preach his word (Mk 3:13-14), to baptize in his name (Mt 28:19), to forgive sins (Jn 20:23), to offer his Body and Blood (Lk 22:19-20), to heal (Mt 10:1). And as Jesus returned to his Father in heaven, he sent these men into the world to continue his work of salvation (Mk 16:15-20).

"I solemnly assure you," Jesus told his disciples, "he who accepts anyone I send accepts me, and in accepting me accepts him who sent me" (Jn 13:20).

It is through Jesus' disciples, and through the

people called together and taught by the disciples, that Jesus remains present in the world. It is through the church that he continues to call people to himself, to save them from sin, to heal the sick and the afflicted.

The Acts of the Apostles presents a model of the church as it should be:

> They devoted themselves to the apostles' instructions and the communal life, to the breaking of bread and the prayers. A reverent fear overtook them all, for many wonders and signs were performed by the apostles. Those who believed shared all things in common; they would sell their property and goods, dividing everything on the basis of each one's need. They went to the temple area together every day, while in their homes they broke bread. With exultant and sincere hearts they took their meals in common, praising God and winning the approval of all the people. Day by day the Lord added to their number those who were being saved. (Acts 2:42-47)

Here we see the power of Jesus, and the power of his Holy Spirit, acting through the church: healings, conversions, signs and wonders, care for the poor, a real community life—all flowing with and from the church's apostolic teaching authority and liturgical life.

It is true that even our most vibrant, most fully renewed parishes fall short of this ideal. The apostolic church itself fell short: If we read the rest of Acts and the New Testament letters, we discover that the early church soon had its own problems of division and confusion and need for renewal. Yet then and now Jesus continues to work through his church despite our human failings. The sacraments of the church, the teaching authority of the bishops, the special prayers and devotions of our tradition—these are all channels by which Jesus himself ministers to us.

When we are baptized, it is Jesus who cleanses us of sin and gives us a new birth in his Spirit. When we are confirmed, it is Jesus who pours out the fullness of the Holy Spirit on us, with all his gifts and power. When we celebrate the Eucharist, it is Jesus who shares his own Body and Blood with us. When we confess our sins and receive absolution, it is Jesus who forgives us. When we celebrate Matrimony or receive Holy Orders, it is Jesus who consecrates us for our special calling. When we receive the Anointing of the Sick, it is Jesus who offers us healing.

Because all the sacraments bring us into contact with Jesus, all the sacraments offer healing on some level. When we examine the actual prayers and liturgies for the sacraments, we discover that the church encourages us to expect God's healing action through these sacred mysteries.

Baptism and Confirmation

The sacraments of Baptism and Confirmation, together with First Communion, are called sacraments of initiation, because they mark the beginning of our new life in Christ. In the early church, when many adult converts were joining the church, the sacraments were administered together—usually at the Easter Vigil liturgy on Holy Saturday night.

Today most Catholics are baptized as infants and receive Confirmation and First Communion later, when they are mature enough to make their own faith commitment. While this practice makes a great deal of sense pastorally, it can keep us from seeing how these sacraments of initiation fit together in the full drama of spiritual rebirth. Our experience of the sacraments gets separated from any experience of conversion, personal change, coming to know Jesus Christ as Lord and Savior—and of course, from any expectation of healing.

Consequently, one of the great challenges facing the church today is that we have many "sacramentalized" Catholics who are not evangelized. There are Catholics with baptismal certificates who do not really seem to know Jesus Christ as their Lord and Savior. There are Catholics with Confirmation certificates who do not know the full power and grace of the Holy Spirit.

In the early church, the time of bringing people into the church was very much a time of conversion, of personal renunciation of sin and Satan, of deep personal commitment to Jesus Christ, and of healing. The church recognized that as we are healed spiritually through Baptism and Confirmation, we are also touched in mind and body by the power of the Holy Spirit.

In the early church, new Christians were anointed with blessed oil just before being baptized and confirmed. We can read some of the early liturgies and writings of the Fathers of the church in *From Darkness to Light: What It Meant to Become a Christian in the Early Church,* by Anne Field, O.S.B. (Ann Arbor, MI: Servant Books, 1978). One of the ancient liturgies included the following prayer:

> We now anoint these servants of yours
> who have come to be born anew
> in this holy sacrament.
> We pray that our Lord Jesus Christ
> may heal and strengthen them.
> May he reveal his power to them,
> through this anointing,
> removing from them every trace of sin and
>   wickedness
> and all the effects of Satan's malice,
> so that they may be cleansed and set free
> in body, soul, and spirit.

The early church fathers also saw a link between Baptism and the biblical accounts of God's healing. In teaching about Baptism, they told of the healing of Naaman, a Syrian official struck by leprosy, who was commanded by the Old Testament prophet Elijah to bathe in the Jordan River (see 2 Kgs 5). They told of the blind man healed when Jesus sent him to wash in the pool of Siloam (see Jn 9:7) and the paralyzed man healed as he lay by the pool of Bethesda, unable to put himself in the water (see Jn 5:1-9). In all of these stories they saw the promise that God will heal body, soul, and spirit through the sacrament of Baptism.

"No one lies unhealed beside the Christian font," wrote one of the Fathers. "Whoever desires to be whole and to receive new life comes to be baptized and is cured. The water is always ready to heal, as soon as anyone comes. Only those who refuse to come remain sick."

In recent years the church has introduced a revised "Rite of Christian Initiation for Adults" (usually abbreviated RCIA), which restores many aspects of the ancient liturgy. Parishes are just now beginning to use the RCIA. I believe that as it gets more fully implemented, it will have a profound impact on our awareness of what God offers us through the sacraments of initiation.

The RCIA speaks of initiation as a process of conversion and commitment to the Lord. The weeks of preparation for the actual sacraments include times for explicit renunciation of sin, for casting out Satan and his evil spirits, for rejecting every form of false worship and every power other than God, for sealing people with the sign of the cross. The whole process is one of continuous transformation, continuous liberation, and continuous healing of body, soul, and spirit.

I would strongly encourage anyone who wants a deeper understanding of the healing power of Baptism and Confirmation to study this new Rite of Christian Initiation for Adults. In closing here, I will offer just one of the prayers that indicates the great spiritual richness of this liturgy:

Lord Jesus,
you are the fountain we thirst for;
you are the teacher we seek;
you alone are the Holy One.
These chosen ones open their hearts honestly
to confess their failures
and be forgiven.
In your love, free them from evil,
restore their health,

satisfy their thirst, and give them peace.
By the power of your name,
which we call upon in faith,
stay with them and save them.
Command the spirit of evil to leave them,
for you have conquered that spirit by rising to life.
Show your chosen people the way of life
   in the Holy Spirit
that they may grow closer to the Father and worship
   him,
for you are Lord for ever and ever.
Amen.

Reconciliation

You only get initiated into something once. Baptism and Confirmation are tremendous experiences of God's grace and healing, but we only receive them once in our lives. Our challenge then is to keep living in the power of our new birth in Jesus.

As all of us know from sad experience, we often fall short. We struggle, we fail, we sin. I spoke in the last chapter of our need for ongoing conversion, ongoing repentance and change—all of which is a part of being open to God's healing power.

The sacrament of Reconciliation, or Penance, is in one sense a renewal of our baptism. When we confess our sins to an ordained priest of the church and receive absolution, the Lord himself forgives us. He restores all the graces of our new birth in his Spirit. This is one of the greatest powers Jesus entrusted to his disciples: "He breathed on them and said, 'Receive the Holy Spirit. If you forgive men's sins, they are forgiven them; if you hold them bound, they are held bound'" (Jn 20:22-23).

Because repentance and forgiveness are so healing in themselves, the sacrament of Reconciliation can be seen as primarily a sacrament of healing. The letter of James urges us, "Declare your sins to one another, and pray for one another, that you may find healing" (Jas 5:16).

Even the church's official instructions for this sacrament speak of healing: "Just as the wound of sin is varied and multiple in the lives of individuals and of the community, so too the healing which Penance provides is varied. Those who, by grave sin, have withdrawn from the communion of love with God are called back with the sacrament of Penance to the life they have lost. Those who through daily weakness fall into venial sins draw strength from a repeated celebration of Penance to gain the full freedom of the children of God."

One of the great joys of my priestly ministry has been to witness God's healing power at work through the sacrament of Reconciliation. I try to leave lots of room for the Spirit to work. As I listen to a person's confession, I also listen for the Spirit, for any inner sense or prompting about problems or needs that go deeper than the person's words. I will take time to share any insight I receive, to pray with the person for healing and change, to offer counsel—all in the context of the sacramental absolution.

On the campus of the Franciscan University of Steubenville, where we celebrate the sacrament in this way and encourage our young men and women to take advantage of it, we see great things happen through

Reconciliation. There is a real growth in holiness that takes place; there are healings of body, soul, and spirit.

Ideally, everyone should be able to celebrate the sacrament of Reconciliation with a priest who understands and believes in its healing dimension. Yet the healing and forgiveness we receive in this sacrament do not come from the priest but from Jesus. If the priest hearing your confession seems abrupt or mechanical, remember that he is only an instrument. Turn with faith to Jesus, repent, accept the words of absolution as Jesus' gift of forgiveness, and expect great things to happen.

The Eucharist

Did you know that every Sunday, at all the masses in all the Catholic churches in the world, millions of people join in prayers for healing?

The fact that most people are surprised by that statement merely shows our lack of attention to the words we pray. For every Catholic immediately recognizes the prayer I am talking about, which the priest and congregation recite together just before Communion:

"Lord, I am not worthy to receive you. But only say the word, and *I shall be healed.*"

As even that one prayer indicates, the Eucharist is truly a sacrament of healing. The Eucharist celebrates our covenant with God—the covenant that frees us from sin and from all the effects of sin, including affliction and death. Through the Eucharist we take part in Jesus' sacrifice of his very life, the sacrifice that has become life and healing for us.

The Eucharist brings us into the most intimate possible contact with Jesus himself. His Blood flows through our veins; his Body becomes one with ours. His mind touches our mind; his very being touches our being. When we enter this moment with real awareness of what is happening and with genuine faith in the Lord's presence, how can it help but be a moment of healing?

The Catholic church officially encourages us to look for healing as we partake of the Lord's Body and Blood. Many of the eucharistic prayers are prayers of healing. Besides the well-known prayer of preparation for Communion mentioned above, consider the priest's own prayer of preparation:

"With faith in your love and mercy I eat your body and drink your blood. Let it not bring me condemnation, but *health in mind and body.*"

Or consider the words a priest prays as he cleans the vessels used for Communion: "Lord, may I receive these gifts in purity of heart. *May they bring me healing and strength,* now and forever."

Consider the prayer that accompanies Holy Communion given outside the Mass by a eucharistic minister: "God our Father, almighty and eternal, we confidently call on you that the Body and the Blood of Jesus Christ, which our brother or sister has received, may *bring him lasting health in mind and body.* We ask this through Christ our Lord."

Once again, I must acknowledge that many Catholic priests and many parish congregations do not celebrate the Eucharist with a real expectation of healing. But the reality of Jesus' presence remains. When we come to the Eucharist with real faith—regardless of the attitudes of others around us—we will encounter the healing presence of the Lord.

One person who gives strong testimony to this truth is Sr. Briege McKenna, a Poor Clare sister from Northern Ireland who now lives in Tampa, Florida. The Lord has given Sister Briege a truly extraordinary gift of healing. She travels around the world to minister at large healing services and retreats. But Sister Briege will tell you that the most ordinary mass celebrated by the most ordinary priest contains a far greater measure of power for healing than any prayer of her own.

"I have seen miracles happen at Mass," she says. "I've seen the blind see. I saw a little boy, nine years of age, who was born deaf and dumb, totally healed when his mother brought him to Mass and Communion. It was an ordinary mass said by an ordinary priest, and the child was healed."

Sister Briege tells of another healing involving an eighteen-year-old girl who had been abandoned on the streets when she was seven. The girl was a prostitute, a heroin addict, and was going blind. She was as hard and bitter a young person as you can possibly imagine.

Some people who wanted to help this girl brought her to a mass where Sister Briege would be speaking.

"She didn't want to be in the church," says Sister Briege. "She thought we were a pack of hypocrites. She didn't listen to a word I said or a word the priest said. But suddenly she began crying—the first time she had cried since she was thirteen—and she couldn't stop.

"When she was walking out the door she said, 'O God, I wish I could believe.' At that moment she had her sight back. She was freed from the heroin as well and never had a moment's withdrawal.

"When I saw her later she said, 'I know what happened. At the moment Christ came, when the bread and wine changed into Jesus, I was changed.'"

This is the power, the reality, the healing love, that is offered to each one of us every time we take part in the Eucharist. A priest who is a friend of mine once told me about a woman who had said to him, "I am not a Catholic. But if I believed what you Catholics say you believe about the Mass, I would *crawl on my knees* to be there every day."

Anointing of the Sick

Anyone who doubts that the Catholic church believes in prayer for healing should consider the fact that the church actually offers a sacrament of healing. In the Anointing of the Sick the church follows the instructions of the letter of James:

"Is there anyone sick among you? He should ask for the presbyters of the church. They in turn are to pray over him, anointing him with oil in the Name [of the Lord]. This prayer uttered in faith will reclaim the one who is ill, and the Lord will restore him to health. If he has committed any sins, forgiveness will be his" (Jas 5:14-15).

Anointing the sick with oil was part of the ministry given by Jesus to his apostles: "Jesus summoned the Twelve and began to send them out two by two, giving them authority over unclean spirits. . . . They expelled many demons, anointed the sick with oil, and worked many cures" (Mk 6:7,13). Since the time of the apostles, the presbyters—or priests—of the church have continued their ministry by anointing the sick with oil in the name of the Lord.

Over the centuries, however, the focus of the
sacrament changed. Rather than a prayer for healing,
the anointing of the sick became primarily a preparation for death. Only the very seriously ill or injured—
those in danger of death—received the sacrament.
People were afraid even to call for a priest, since his
appearance with the blessed oil meant death was near.
And so the sacrament of healing came to be celebrated
only when all hope for healing was gone.

In recent years the church has worked to restore an
understanding of the Anointing of the Sick as a true
sacrament of healing. The revised liturgy for anointing
offers various options: one is a prayer for someone
near death, but others are prayers for healing and
recovery. Many parishes now offer regular group
celebrations of the sacrament for all who are sick or
infirm. And as more priests and deacons celebrate the
sacrament of Anointing with faith in its power for
healing, healings are taking place.

"Since I have discovered that the effect of the
sacrament is to heal, I have witnessed healings," one
priest wrote to us at the Franciscan University of
Steubenville. "For the first twenty-six years of my
priesthood, I didn't know God did that."

One young woman I know went to her doctor
because she was having a buzzing sensation in her ear.
The doctor could not find any explanation for the
buzzing and ordered a CAT scan, an X-ray of the
brain. The CAT scan showed a tumor over the left ear.
It was a type of tumor that cannot be treated and is
always terminal.

This was shattering news for my friend Stephanie
and her husband Marshall. Many Christian brothers

and sisters joined them in praying for Stephanie's healing. The doctor scheduled Stephanie for a second CAT scan. The day before it was to take place, their pastor, a good friend of mine, celebrated the sacrament of Anointing, praying in faith that Stephanie would be healed.

The scan the next day showed no trace of the tumor that had shown clearly in the earlier test. The puzzled doctors could only suggest that the first test was misinterpreted. But in any case they could not explain why the buzzing in Stephanie's ear, the original symptom of trouble, had also disappeared completely.

The prayer with which our bishops consecrate the special blessed oil to be used in anointing the sick expresses the church's faith that healings like Stephanie's will indeed take place as we reach out to Jesus through this sacrament:

Lord God, loving Father,
you bring healing to the sick
through your Son, Jesus Christ.
Hear us as we pray to you in faith.
Send the Holy Spirit,
man's helper and friend,
upon this oil which nature has provided
to serve the needs of men.
May your blessing come upon all
who are anointed with this oil,
that they may be freed from pain and illness,
and made well again in body, mind, and soul.
Father, may this oil be blessed for our use
in the name of our Lord Jesus Christ,
who lives and reigns with you forever.

Matrimony and Holy Orders

In the sacraments of Matrimony and Holy Orders, the Lord consecrates people for specific ministries in his body: the ministry of family life and the ministry of the priesthood. The liturgies for these sacraments do not include specific prayer for healing, yet it is important to see that both sacraments equip God's people to be ministers of healing.

In family life a husband and wife minister God's healing love to each other and to their children. The Christian family is a "little church." This is where the church's life first becomes real to us: this is where God's healing should take place. Matrimony consecrates the love of a husband and wife to become a source of healing and strength for them and their children.

Today, sadly, many homes are not places of healing. Divorce, child abuse, alcoholism, abusive spouses—all these problems in our homes are literally destroying the children who are supposed to be healed and strengthened and nourished in the family. How important it is for Catholic husbands and wives to realize the power and grace of their sacramental bond, so that they can become true ministers of healing!

Holy Orders consecrates men to the special ministries of the priesthood and diaconate. It empowers these men to celebrate all of the other sacraments—to be themselves sacramental signs of Jesus' presence in the church. Now that we have seen the healing dimension contained in all the other sacraments, we realize just how much a Catholic priest is truly a minister of God's healing.

Not long ago I took part in the ordination of a deacon. As I watched the young man prostrating himself before the altar, consecrating his life to the Lord and to the church, I was moved to pray that the Holy Spirit would manifest his power to him. I asked that he would experience the Spirit's presence in such a way that he would realize fully the tremendous power entrusted to him as a deacon of the church.

As I prayed, to my surprise, the young man did in fact experience signs of the Spirit's power and began shaking like a leaf as he felt the great power of God flowing into him, equipping him to minister life and healing to others. How wonderful it would be if at every ordination signs of the Holy Spirit's presence and action were manifest, awakening young men to a full realization of the awesome power entrusted to them in sharing the priesthood of Jesus!

Power for the Church

How is it that we so often overlook or take for granted the tremendous graces for healing and spiritual transformation that Jesus offers us through the sacraments? How is it that we overlook the power of many other gifts of our Catholic heritage?

In recent years I have personally come to a far deeper awareness of the church's sacramentals. Sacramentals are special objects and gestures that have been blessed by the Catholic church to become signs of God's grace and protection. Holy water, blessed candles, blessed oil and salt, rosaries, crucifixes, the sign of the cross—all of these are sacramentals.

Sacramentals carry spiritual power because they are

backed by the faith and prayers of the church. When we use sacramentals in our prayer, we express the fact that we are members of the church, that we have the support and spiritual strength of the entire body of Christ behind us.

Sacramentals are often used in special blessings, as a way of consecrating a person or place for the Lord. They are used to combat the presence of Satan, invoking the prayers of the whole church against the powers of darkness. And they are used for healing.

The sign of the cross, for example, which Catholics so often make mechanically, is a power-filled sign of our consecration to Jesus. The Rite of Christian Initiation for Adults includes a special ceremony in which the priest makes the sign of the cross on those who are moving into deeper life with Jesus. "Receive the cross on your forehead," the priest prays. "By this sign of his triumph, Christ will be your strength. Learn now to know and follow him."

Each time we enter a church and make the sign of the cross with holy water, we renew our baptism. Each time parents make the sign of the cross over their children, they claim those children for the Lord. There is real spiritual power that comes from the sacramental of the sign of the cross. In the same way, holy water, blessed oil, blessed salt, and all the other sacramentals can help us pray for God's protection, strength, and healing.

Perhaps the most striking testimonies I have heard to God's work through sacramentals are those from Fr. Rick Thomas, a Jesuit priest who leads a community that serves the very poor of El Paso, Texas, and Juarez, Mexico.

Fr. Thomas blesses water and oil and salt literally by the gallon. At the community's camp for poor children, he even blesses all the water in the swimming pool, which must make it the world's largest holy water font. Then he and his coworkers pray with children as they are playing in the pool. Great miracles of healing and deliverance and conversion take place in Fr. Thomas's community through prayer backed by the power of the church's sacramentals.

Awakening the Church

Often in this chapter I have been forced to admit the gap between the faith for healing expressed in the official Catholic prayers and teachings and the amount of expectant faith manifest in actual Catholic life. With many other Catholics who have experienced the fruits of renewal, I find it only too easy to get frustrated and judgmental about the church's present condition. Yet I have also learned that frustration and eagerness to judge stem from my own impatience and lack of faith, rather than from the Lord.

It is up to the Lord, after all, to renew his church and awaken his people to all the riches of their heritage. I have been amazed at what he can do when I stop complaining and criticizing other people's faith and offer myself humbly to the Lord to serve in his plan for renewal.

I learned many lessons in church renewal during my years as pastor of St. Joseph's Parish in Little Falls, New York. The parish has a strong Italian heritage, and most of the parishioners had grown up in a very traditional practice of the faith, with a strong emphasis on devotions and saints. I was eager to introduce people to a personal relationship with Jesus, the power of the Holy Spirit, and healing. It took me a little while to learn that all I had to do was help them see the full dimensions of the faith they were already living.

I arrived in the parish just before the feast of St. Rocco—or as most people in the parish called him, St. Rock. For many Italian Catholics, the feast of St. Rock is a major celebration. The older ladies of the parish had no sooner met me than they began explaining what I had to do for the feast of St. Rock.

Although I am of Italian descent, I knew very little about St. Rock. And some of the ladies' instructions did not sit quite right with me. For one, they wanted to put a statue of St. Rock in the middle of the sanctuary, where I felt it would distract from our focus on the central reality of the eucharistic celebration. So I was less than enthusiastic about the whole festival—until I looked up St. Rock in some reference books.

The more I read, the more excited I became. St. Rock was a young Frenchman of the Middle Ages who was converted by the preaching of one of the popes. He followed the pope back to Rome, then stayed in Italy as a pilgrim, telling others about the Lord. Today we would call Rock a lay evangelist; wherever he went, many people were converted through his preaching.

This was at a time when great plagues were ravaging Europe. Rock began ministering to the sick—even when he himself was struck by the plague—and many were healed through his prayers. According to the story, one of those healed turned out to be the pope's brother. The pope then gave Rock permission to continue his ministry of evangelism and healing.

When Rock finally returned to his home in France, he had been gone so long that no one recognized him. The local governor decided he was an Italian spy and threw him in jail, where he died. But after his death, as the story of Rock's life spread, people continued to ask for his prayers, and especially for his intercession for healing. We could really consider St. Rock one of the patrons of the healing ministry.

I decided to use the feast of St. Rock to help my parishioners understand the power for healing contained in their Catholic faith and traditions. I went back to the ladies and told them I would like to make a few changes in the celebration.

"Let's have a special mass and a big party afterward," I said. "I want to leave the statue in its regular place, but we'll have some special prayers after the mass and pray especially for anyone who is sick." Everyone seemed satisfied with this proposal, and the preparations got underway.

The day of the big celebration, I drove over to the Italian bakery in a nearby town to pick up things for the parish party. As I was collecting our order, a young man tapped me on the shoulder.

"Are you Fr. Bertolucci?" he asked.

The young man's name was Mark, and he had recognized me because he was active in the Catholic charismatic renewal. We talked for a few minutes, and a plan started forming in my mind.

"Mark, we're having a big mass at my parish tonight for the feast of St. Rock. Would you come and after Communion tell everyone what Jesus Christ has come to mean to you?"

Mark's eyes lit up.

"I'd love to, Father," he answered. And so we were set.

The church was packed that evening. Everyone had heard that the new pastor was trying something different for the feast of St. Rock. I had selected Scripture readings that spoke of healing, and in my sermon I spoke of Rock as a young man who had given his life to the Lord Jesus Christ. I told how he had prayed with people for healing and how God answered his prayers.

"Why did St. Rock pray with people for healing?" I asked them. "Because Jesus prayed with people for healing. And Jesus told his disciples to pray with people for healing. The church still wants us to pray for healing, and that is why the church holds St. Rock up to us as a model.

"I've invited a young man here today who is the age St. Rock was when he ministered, " I added. "And he too has had a powerful experience of Jesus. He'll tell you all about it after Communion."

So Mark stood up after Communion and told how Jesus Christ had come into his life, what Jesus meant to him personally, and how he had learned to pray with people that they too might experience Jesus more deeply.

When Mark sat down, I took the microphone.

"As you know, we'll be having a big party in the basement here after mass," I said. "So please, when mass is finished, feel free to go on downstairs for the celebration. But Mark and I will stay here in the church for a little while, and we will be happy to pray with anyone who would like—just as St. Rock used to pray with people."

Mark and I ended up praying with many people that night. Practically the whole congregation came up for prayer. These tradition-minded Catholics had never done anything like it before in their lives. But once they understood that prayer for healing was really a part of their Catholic faith, they were ready.

The next Sunday a number of people came back to the sacristy to ask me to pray with them for various problems. One of the ushers who had been ailing asked for prayer. He was not completely healed, but there was enough immediate improvement in his condition that someone else noticed. Word raced through the parish. By the next week, there was a line of people outside the sacristy asking for prayer.

My experience at St. Joseph's helped to open my eyes to the spiritual power already present in the devotions, prayers, sacramentals, and sacraments of our Catholic faith. The renewal of the healing ministry should not be seen as a departure in any way from Catholic tradition, but only as a greater awakening to realities that are already there.

SIX

When We
Are Not Healed

D ANNY WAS A GOOD FRIEND OF MINE.
I had known this young man from his early
teens. He came from a wonderful Catholic family here
in Steubenville. His parents were people of deep faith,
who truly loved the Lord and their children. They were
a great support to other Christian families as well.

When Danny was fifteen, he developed cancer—a
brain tumor.

We all prayed and fasted for Danny's healing. The
priests of our Steubenville community ministered to
him with complete faith in God's power to heal
through the sacraments. The surgery to remove the
cancer was far more successful than the doctors had
expected, and Danny recovered well. We all rejoiced
that God had heard our prayers and Danny had been
healed.

Then, after a very few years, the cancer returned.

There was more prayer, more ministry, more surgery and medication. But the cancer cells continued to
spread. Finally my young friend Danny died.

Why?

If Danny's family and friends believed that God wants to heal and deliver us from affliction . . .

If we turned to the Lord through all the various channels of healing he offers, including deeper conversion and repentance . . .

If we trusted in Jesus' healing presence in the sacraments . . .

If we followed all the principles this book has presented—then why did Danny die? Why do other faithful Christians, young and old, continue to suffer sickness and affliction even though they turn to God for healing?

Why doesn't healing always happen?

Does God Guarantee Healing?

Most of us have encountered Christians who claim that healing *will* always happen, that God will always grant what we request so long as we have enough faith. This approach puts a heavy burden of guilt on those who do not experience physical healing. They wonder how they have failed in their faith. They may worry that God is punishing them for some sin they had forgotten about or don't even realize they committed. They may finally decide God has abandoned them, that he does not honor his promises, that they cannot trust God.

Anyone who has read this far knows that I believe in healing. I believe in miracles. I believe in the importance of faith in opening the way for God's healing touch in our lives. I would like to see the whole church expect and experience far more power for healing.

Yet I would also stress that the Lord has not guaranteed to give us physical healing every time we ask. Nothing in the Word of God tells us that Jesus promised to eradicate all suffering and death from our lives before his second coming. Quite the contrary.

In his first appearance among us, Jesus inaugurated the messianic era, in which the power of sin would be defeated and God's reign over human life restored. He came as a suffering Messiah, taking upon himself all the pain and affliction sin had introduced into human life. He offered us new strength to live in obedience to him through all the trials and difficulties of our present life.

But Jesus also told us that his victory would not be complete until he comes again. Then he will come as a victorious king to sweep away the remnants of evil and restore the fullness of God's kingdom on earth. Then everything that causes suffering and deterioration and affliction in human life will pass away.

The promise of God's kingdom breaks through in our lives even now, in miracles and healings that offer us a foretaste of Jesus' final victory. It is right that we ask for miracles and expect to see them happen, for Jesus wants his kingdom to shine forth in our midst. We also give witness to the coming kingdom by sharing in the Lord's creative work. Every advance in medical science, every advance in technology to improve human life, every advance in curing illness, is a sign and promise of the new heaven and the new earth.

But we have no guarantee, in this messianic age between the first coming of the Lord and his coming again, that all suffering, sickness, disease, and death will vanish from our lives. We still wait in hope for the appearance of our victorious king. We are on the way, but we are not there yet.

We see this even in the life of the apostolic church. The apostle Paul worked many miracles, including healings. Yet Paul's letters also speak of times when he or his coworkers were not healed, or when they recovered only after an extended period of sickness.

"You are aware that it was a bodily ailment that first occasioned my bringing you the gospel," Paul wrote to the Galatians (4:13). "Trophimus I had to leave ill at Miletus," he wrote of one co-worker (2 Tm 4:20), and of another, "[Epaphroditus] was, in fact, sick to the point of death" (Phil 2:27).

For Paul such afflictions were part of the suffering and difficulties he bore joyfully for the sake of the gospel. "As I see it," he wrote in one letter, "God has put us apostles at the end of the line, like men doomed to die in the arena. . . . Up to this very hour we go hungry and thirsty, poorly clad, roughly treated, wandering about homeless. We work hard at manual labor. When we are insulted we respond with a blessing. Persecution comes our way; we bear it patiently. We are slandered, and we try conciliation. We have become the world's refuse, the scum of all; that is the present state of affairs" (1 Cor 4:9, 11-13).

I wonder what Paul would have to say to some of the television evangelists who promise unlimited prosperity, health, and material blessings? Yet wasn't Paul's experience closer to the example given by Jesus himself? Jesus did not run away from pain and suffering and death: he embraced them, he accepted them, and he turned them into victory.

I believe this is the key to understanding and responding when we do not receive a physical healing. Jesus does not promise us a life free of suffering. But he does promise us a victory that can be found in the midst of our suffering.

Spiritual Healing

When we speak of people who are not healed, we must remember a point I have stressed many times in this book: Healing takes place on more than one level.

Our human nature has three dimensions: body, soul, and spirit. As St. Paul prayed, "May the God of peace make you perfect in holiness. May he preserve you whole and entire, spirit, soul, and body, irreproachable at the coming of our Lord Jesus Christ" (1 Thes 5:23). Healing touches all three levels. The healing of our bodies we call physical or physiological healing. The healing of the soul is emotional or psychological healing. Healing also has a spiritual dimension: when we are freed from sin, when we grow in love and trust of God, we experience spiritual healing.

People are naturally eager to see healings on the physical level first, and perhaps then on the psychological level. Healings of our body and emotions touch the areas where we most directly feel the pain and anguish of our human condition. We hurt physically, we hurt emotionally, and we want the hurt to stop.

The Lord wants to heal us at all levels of our being—body, soul, and spirit. Yet clearly, from his perspective, the most important dimension of healing is the spiritual. "What profit does a man show who gains the whole world and destroys himself in the process?" Jesus asked (Mk 8:36). And what profit do we ourselves show if we enjoy perfect physical health and a wonderful self-image, yet remain cut off from the very source of life, the Lord himself?

Very often when I have ministered to those who are sick, I have not seen a change on the physical level. But

I have definitely seen spiritual transformations every bit as real as any physical miracle. People who were terrified of death and of pain have been strengthened to bear sufferings with joy. People full of bitterness and anger have been healed and filled with love. People who had wandered far from God have turned back to him with faith and trust.

This is true spiritual healing, true restoration of a life and strength that will never perish.

I spoke above of my young friend Danny, who died despite all of our prayers for healing. Yet Danny and all of us who loved him did not experience his death as a defeat. We had seen him grow stronger and closer to the Lord even as his illness progressed. He died victoriously, in the peace of the Lord, surrounded by his loved ones, comforted by the sacraments of the church, ready to face his loving Father.

After ministering to many people like Danny, I have come to consider it something of a mistake to speak of "those who are not healed." If our prayers for healing have drawn us back to the Lord in a deeper conversion, if we have repented of sins and unfaithfulness, if we have grown in faith and trust, if we have been nourished by the Lord through his sacraments—how can we say we have not been healed?

Redemptive Suffering

I have spoken of suffering and sickness as an evil God did not intend for human life, an evil we experience because of sin. Yet when we study our heritage of Catholic spiritual teaching and the lives of the men and women recognized by the church as saints, we often find suffering presented as a means of holiness and spiritual growth. A number of saints endured long, painful illnesses and embraced all those sufferings as a sign of God's work in their lives.

If suffering and sickness were not God's plan for us in the first place, how can suffering and sickness possibly have spiritual value?

The answer leads us back to the central mystery of God's plan to save us from sin and all its consequences. God conquered pain and death by embracing them in the person of his incarnate Son, Jesus Christ. On the cross, dying the painful, shameful death of a criminal, Jesus turned the very evils that had entered human life through sin into the means of our salvation.

Jesus warned his disciples that they too would suffer in this life. But he also promised that they would share his victory through their suffering.

"You will suffer in the world," Jesus said. "But take courage! I have overcome the world" (Jn 16:33).

Suffering and sickness and pain have no value in themselves. They are destructive; they diminish God's gift of life. Yet Jesus can give our suffering meaning and value. Whether we suffer directly for our faith through persecution or suffer because of sickness and afflictions, the Lord can turn our anguish into a source of strength and salvation.

"Even now I find my joy in the sufferings I endure for you," wrote Paul. "In my own flesh I fill up whatever is lacking in the sufferings of Christ for the sake of his body, the church" (Col 1:24). Paul had learned to join his suffering to the sufferings of Jesus; he had entered into the mystery of Jesus' sacrifice for the church. This is why the Eucharist becomes so

meaningful in times of pain: suffering helps us pene-
trate to the very heart of Jesus' sacrifice.

In my own thinking, I have come to make a
distinction between sickness itself and the suffering
that accompanies sickness. I regard sickness as an evil
which we are always to fight, a sign that we still await
the Lord's full victory over all the effects of human sin.
As Paul writes, " ... we know that all creation groans
and is in agony even until now. Not only that, but we
ourselves, although we have the Spirit as first fruits,
groan inwardly while we await the redemption of our
bodies" (Rom 8:22-23). When Jesus comes again,
there will be no more sickness and suffering in the new
world he will bring about: "He shall wipe every tear
from their eyes, and there shall be no more death or
mourning, crying out or pain, for the former world
has passed away" (Rv 21:4).

Yet the suffering that we experience through sickness can become redemptive, take on value, as we
consciously join it with the sufferings of Christ. When
I would visit my young friend Danny during his
struggle with cancer, I would always pray for a healing.
I would always pray for a miracle. But I also talked to
him about the promise on the other side of suffering.

"God loves you, Danny," I would tell him. "I'm sure
of that. So just take all this suffering, and all the
physical pain, and all the hurt of being fifteen years old
and not able to play sports or go to school or run
around with your friends—take it all and give it to
Jesus. Join it to the Lord's suffering, the Lord's cross.
Ask the Lord to use your suffering for you, for your
family, for all of us who care about you. Ask the Lord
to use it for the church, for the world. And then see
what happens!"

We discovered later that at the very hour of Danny's death, a friend of one of his brothers was healed of a blood disorder and received the grace of conversion to the Lord. Danny had been asked to pray for this person by offering his suffering in union with Jesus.

Comfort the Sick

It is not always easy for healthy people to be around people who are sick or severely handicapped. The sight of another person's suffering stirs many uncomfortable feelings of fear, helplessness, guilt, even anger.

As we reflect on the reality of sickness and suffering and pain in our own lives, we are challenged to examine our attitudes toward sickness in others. Jesus himself, by his own example, taught us to reach out to the sick in love—caring for them, easing their suffering, leading them to the healing love of the Father.

Jesus told his disciples that at the Last Judgment all nations would be divided according to how they had responded to his presence in his "least brothers." "I was ill and you comforted me," the king says to the just as they enter their reward. "Lord, when did we visit you when you were ill?" they ask him. And he answers, "I assure you, as often as you did it for one of my least brothers, you did it for me" (see Mt 25:31-40).

"I was ill and you comforted me." Note that Jesus does not say, "I was ill and you healed me." Whether or not our sick brothers and sisters experience physical healing through our ministry, we are called to continue caring for them, to continue comforting them, to keep them surrounded with faith and with love.

This was the kind of love the apostle Paul experienced from his fellow Christians during the illness he mentioned in the letter to the Galatians. "My physical condition was a challenge which you did not despise or brush aside in disgust," Paul wrote. "On the contrary, you took me to yourselves as an angel of God, even as if I had been Christ Jesus!" (Gal 4:14).

How do we measure in our love for the sick? Do we let ourselves be repulsed by the ugliness of sickness, and so brush aside or run away from people who need our comfort and love? Do we welcome the sick and the handicapped into our parishes and families as we would welcome Jesus himself?

We are called to serve those who are suffering. We are called to serve those who do not experience physical healing when we lay hands on them and pray with them. We are called to reach out to people in sanatoriums and hospitals and nursing homes, to those who are retarded or severely deformed, to those who may have to endure tremendous physical suffering all their lives.

God has something to say to them too. God is reaching out to them through our hands to bring them salvation from their anguish. In our love and care and faith, they can find meaning and worth. They can experience spiritual transformation and spiritual healing. They can receive courage, knowing that their lives are not wasted or lacking in value.

In a very real sense these brothers and sisters are Jesus for us. This is the reality Mother Teresa of Calcutta so often speaks of in her ministry to the abandoned and suffering: "Jesus in the distressing disguise of the poor." In pain, in sickness, in deformity, we meet Jesus, who has entered into our suffering so that we can enter into glory.

SEVEN

Death

I T IS THE ONE REALITY IN LIFE WE MOST DREAD.
We ignore it. We act as if we will never face it. We invent all kinds of euphemisms to avoid even saying the word. And yet it is the one reality we can never escape.

Death.

The cold inescapable fact is that you and I and all our loved ones—and indeed, every human being upon the earth—will die.

We find it so hard even to imagine death—to think of ceasing to be, of never again feeling the sun or seeing the sky or hearing laughter. We cannot imagine the world going on without us. We find it so difficult to bear the death of a loved one, to know we will never again see that familiar face or hear that special voice.

What a terrible, awesome, fearsome thing is death.

And yet, for us who are Christians, this fearsome reality of death has become a promise of joy, healing, consolation, and hope. Because for us death represents not the grim end of existence but the doorway to a new and eternal life.

The New Testament speaks of death simply as "falling asleep in the Lord." The apostle Paul can honestly say of life and death, "I do not know which to prefer" (Phil 1:22). Catholic tradition regards a happy death as one of the greatest gifts God can give. The church actually has a prayer we can pray daily for the grace of a happy death.

That is why a book on the healing ministry needs to include a chapter on death and its meaning for us as Christians. For death does not represent a defeat for God's healing power—"Why did God let my friend die rather than heal her?" Rather, it is in death that we find the ultimate healing, for through death we go home to the Lord, who will wipe every tear from our eyes.

The Seed of Eternity

Even though a Christian can contemplate death with hope, we recognize that death is not something good in itself. Our God is a God of life; he never wanted death as part of his creation. As with sickness, death resulted from Satan's efforts to corrupt and destroy God's gift of life.

"God did not make death," the Scriptures tell us, "nor does he rejoice in the destruction of the living. . . For God formed man to be imperishable; the image of his own nature he made him. But by the envy of the devil, death entered the world, and they who are in his possession experience it" (Wis 1:13; 2:23-24).

Every human being who has ever lived was created to be imperishable, to live forever. Part of our difficulty in accepting death reflects an instinctive knowledge that we were not meant just to vanish from existence. The Catholic bishops at the Second Vatican Council spoke of this truth: "But a deep instinct leads (man) rightly to shrink from and to reject the utter ruin and total loss of his personality. Because he bears in himself the seed of eternity, which cannot be reduced to mere matter, he rebels against death" (*The Church in the Modern World,* p. 18).

I myself have ministered to dying people who were not believers, and I have seen in their final moments a kind of inner awareness that there has to be more, that the human spirit does not simply disappear with the death of our bodies. We know instinctively that we are meant to live forever.

Yet our instinctive rejection of death is not enough to save us. The only one who can save us from death is Jesus Christ, who died yet rose again, and who promises to raise us up as well.

Long before Jesus appeared on this earth, the prophet Isaiah was inspired by the Holy Spirit to see that God desired to save the human race from death:

"On this mountain," proclaimed Isaiah, "he will destroy the veil that veils all peoples, the web that is woven over all nations; he will destroy death forever. The Lord God will wipe away the tears from all faces; the reproach of his people he will remove from the whole earth" (Is 25:7-8).

Now, in Jesus, the prophecy of Isaiah is fulfilled: "If death began its reign through one man because of his offense [our first father, Adam], much more shall those who receive the overflowing grace and gift of justice live and reign through the one man, Jesus Christ" (Rom 5:17).

Life after Death

What does the promise of eternal life mean for us as followers of Jesus today? We know that we still face the inevitability of physical death. But what happens after our physical death? What is the mystery that takes place when someone breathes his last?

The full answer to that question is something we do not know and cannot know. Scripture tells us, "Eye has not seen, ear has not heard, nor has it so much as dawned on man what God has prepared for those who love him" (1 Cor 2:9). But we do know that when the physical life process stops, the human person goes on. Even as I see the body placed in the grave, the real person I knew continues to exist.

The Catholic church has traditionally used the word *soul* to speak of that part of us that survives and continues after death. As I have discussed elsewhere in this book, the word *soul* can have other scriptural meanings when we speak of "body, soul, and spirit." But the church also uses this term to describe the essential element of the human self, endowed with individual consciousness and will, that does not die.

In my own priestly ministry I have been blessed at times with a very clear sense that a person's soul—the real self—was still alive even as I witnessed the death of the body.

As a parish pastor in the town of Little Falls, New York, I often visited an elderly couple named Dominick and Adelina. Adelina was in her eighties, and her health was failing. She sometimes said to me, "Father John, when it's time for me to go home, I want you here to pray with me."

Then one day, only a short time after I had been at their home to bring them Holy Communion, I received a call that Adelina had suffered a heart attack at home. An emergency unit had rushed her to the hospital, but she was declared dead on her arrival.

I felt very bad that I had not been able to fulfill Adelina's wish for me to be with her and pray with her as she died. As soon as I could, I went to the hospital morgue so I could at least say a prayer over her body.

When I pulled back the sheet and placed my hand on Adelina's shoulder to pray, I was surprised to find the warmth of life still present, even though she had been pronounced dead some time before. I felt very strongly that Adelina was still there, that her soul had not yet left her body but was waiting for her pastor.

I prayed the prayers of the church, the special blessing for the moment of death. And as I finished my prayer, Adelina went on to the Lord. Almost in an instant the warmth left her body. Suddenly my hands were touching a cold, lifeless corpse, where only moments before there had been a living warmth.

Adelina had waited for me to pray with her as she journeyed home to the Father. And in waiting she allowed me to have an unforgettable experience of the truth that our life goes on even as our bodies perish. Other pastors have shared with me similar experiences of feeling a person's living presence in the room even as they stood beside the lifeless body. Death is not the end; it is only a passing from one life to the next.

Preparing for Death

When we are uncomfortable with the thought of death, we tend to put off any kind of preparation for it. On a purely practical level, people will put off writing a will, even though they risk creating serious financial and legal problems for their families. On a spiritual level, many people put off preparing to meet the Lord until they are on their deathbeds. In fact, one still finds families waiting till the very last moment even to call a priest to minister to a dying relative, for fear of alarming the sick person.

Yet no matter how healthy a person may be, no matter how far away death seems, we must always be prepared. And the best preparation for death is to live fully for the Lord Jesus Christ right now. When our life truly centers upon Jesus, when he matters more to us than anything else, then death becomes almost a matter of indifference. For death will only bring us closer to him.

Paul experienced this truth, and wrote in his letter to the Philippians, "To me, 'life' means Christ; hence dying is so much gain" (Phil 1:21). Because Jesus had become Paul's whole life, he had nothing to fear from death. On the contrary, he could look forward to death with joy: "Dying is so much gain."

Yet we should not imagine Paul waking up every morning wishing he were dead. His life on this earth brought joy as well, for it gave him the opportunity to serve the Lord he loved: "If, on the other hand, I am to go on living in the flesh, that means productive toil for me" (Phil 1:22). For Paul, both life and death were full of promise, which left him in an interesting predicament: "I do not know which to prefer. I am strongly attracted by both. I long to be freed from this life and to be with Christ, for that is the far better thing; yet it is more urgent that I remain alive for your sakes" (Phil 1:22-24).

In these words of Paul we see a man truly prepared for death. Paul would have been happy to die the next minute or to live for another hundred years. He had reached a point of balance, a point of freedom, where he could face the inevitable reality of death with complete peace. And the only secret to Paul's peace of mind was that he had made Jesus his whole life.

Food for the Way

We prepare for death first of all by the way we live—by living in and for and through Jesus. But the Lord has also given us more specific helps to strengthen and support us when we come to the actual moment of dying. Perhaps the most important of these is the gift of his very own Body and Blood as the food that sustains us on our final journey.

"He who feeds on my flesh and drinks my blood has life eternal, and I will raise him up on the last day" (Jn 6:54). The Catholic church has always taken these words of Jesus very literally and very seriously. The Body and Blood of the Lord is the guarantee of our covenant with God, like the sacrificial lamb of the Passover meal which sealed God's covenant with the people of Israel. In the Eucharist we receive the true Body and Blood of Jesus under the appearance of bread and wine. "For my flesh is real food and my blood real drink," Jesus assures us. "The man who feeds on my flesh and drinks my blood remains in me, and I in him" (Jn 6:55-56).

The final Communion given to a dying person marks a special moment of grace and strength. The church calls this last sacrament of one's life *Viaticum,* a Latin word which literally means "on the way with you." In that very powerful and precious moment of passing over to the Lord, the sacrament marks the presence of Jesus, who travels "on the way" with us.

The celebration of *Viaticum* usually involves more than simply receiving Communion. First the priest leads the dying person to a deeper repentance and renunciation of sin. If the person is able, he will make a confession of his sins and wrongdoings. Then the priest, exercising the authority Jesus gave to his apostles to forgive sins (see Jn 20:23), will pronounce the church's absolution: "Through the holy mysteries of our redemption, may almighty God release you from all punishments in this life and in the life to come. May he open to you the gates of paradise, and welcome you to everlasting joy."

What a great gift this represents for us: to be reconciled with God and assured of his forgiveness as we prepare to meet him face to face!

Then follows a brief reading and reflection upon the Scriptures, so that the dying person and all the family and friends present may be nourished and strengthened by the Word of God. The passage I most often use when ministering *Viaticum* is that same verse from John's Gospel mentioned above: "He who feeds on my flesh and drinks my blood has life eternal, and I will raise him up on the last day" (Jn 6:54). Here we have another great gift: to know in our final moments that Jesus has given us his assurance of eternal life, sealed with the sign of his Body and Blood.

Next the priest leads the dying person in a renewal of baptismal promises. Baptism itself is a sign of dying and new life: we die to sin and self, and we are raised up to a new life in Jesus Christ. As we approach the moment of physical death, the renewal of our baptismal vows is another assurance of the eternal life that awaits us.

Finally comes the celebration of Communion itself. All those present pray together the Lord's Prayer—the prayer Jesus himself gave us, reminding us that our God is truly a loving Father. The priest then shares the Eucharist with these beautiful words: "Jesus Christ is the food for our journey. He calls us to the heavenly table. This is the Bread of Life: taste, and see that the Lord is good."

The person who is about to receive Communion repeats those ancient words derived from the Scripture: "Lord, I am not worthy to receive you, but only say the word and I shall be healed" (see Mt 8:8). The priest gives Communion and says, "May the Lord Jesus Christ protect you and lead you to eternal life."

This is *Viaticum*, "on the way with you." This is food for the journey, the pledge of resurrection. I have outlined the prayers and ritual of this great sacramental moment because I know many people dread what should be a precious, healing experience. I have seen people walk out of the sick room as I prepared to minister, because they could not face the reality *Viaticum* expresses. Or people will delay calling for a priest until the last possible moment—sometimes until it is really too late.

Yet how little there is to fear, and how much comfort and peace the Lord offers us through this final assurance that he himself will go "on the way with us" as we travel that final journey to his Father.

Ministering to the Dying

As we learn to face our own death without fear, we also become free to minister lovingly to those who are dying. After all, most of us will be touched by many deaths before we ourselves die—parents, friends, relatives, perhaps our spouse. The most loving final gift we can offer is to help them prepare to meet death with confidence and hope.

In recent years we have made great advances in helping people prepare for death on two fronts: the physical and the psychological. Medical science has made great advances in prolonging life with new treatments for heart disease, for some cancers, and for other illnesses. At the same time, doctors are becoming more sensitive in recognizing when they can no longer fight death but should concentrate on easing physical pain and helping the patient prepare for death. Psychologists and psychiatrists have also learned a great deal about how to help the dying person and the family cope with the emotional trauma of approaching death.

Yet all of that wisdom, important as it is, addresses only two dimensions of the human person. It does not help us to prepare on a very necessary third level: the level of the spirit. When I minister to a dying person, I am concerned above all else to help that person prepare spiritually for the reality of death. I want to do all I can to lead that person closer to Jesus, for only Jesus can offer him eternal life.

The best service you can render to those you love as they approach the moment of death is to be sure they are right with God. We need a special sensitivity in this: a sick, possibly pain-wracked person usually won't appreciate hard-sell evangelism. Simply being present, offering to pray, speaking about Jesus—such simple, loving words and actions can have a profound impact at this critical time.

People who face death often want to talk about the Lord. They may feel a need to resolve wrongdoing and unforgiven hurts. You may find them more open now than ever before to the truth of the gospel. Don't be afraid to be with them and to listen to them and pray with them. Don't hesitate to call in the elders of the church to minister the sacraments.

Ministry to the dying should really rank as a part of the healing ministry—perhaps the greatest of the healing ministries. For even the most total, miraculous physical healing is only temporary; even Lazarus, whom Jesus raised from the dead, eventually had to die. But when we come to that inevitable moment prepared—reconciled with God, nourished by the Eucharist, strengthened in faith by the gospel—death itself becomes a doorway to the ultimate healing we all long for and need.

Mourning

When our brothers and sisters in the Lord die, we can rejoice for them, knowing as we do that they are on their way to the joy of heaven. Yet those of us left behind cannot help but feel great sorrow and loss as well. Weeping and grieving for the dead is a normal experience, even for one who believes in the promise of eternal life.

Christians sometimes make the mistake of thinking that any great display of grief for a loved one shows some lack of faith. Nothing could be further from the truth. Simply because we are human, we need to mourn, to cry, to work through the great pain of separation from the one we love. Tears can be healing for our grief, and to repress or stifle our tears can make us very sick indeed.

Anyone who doubts what I say need only look at the example of Jesus himself, who stood by the tomb of his friend Lazarus and wept. Jesus had come to raise Lazarus from the dead; moments before he had assured Lazarus's sister Martha, "I am the resurrection and the life; whoever believes in me, though he should die, will come to life; and whoever is alive and believes in me will never die" (Jn 11:25-26). Yet here among the mourners, confronted with the reality of his friend's death, seeing the tears of Mary and Martha, Jesus "was troubled in spirit, moved by the deepest emotions" (Jn 11:33). As they led him to the tomb, "Jesus began to weep" (Jn 11:35).

Tears, sorrow, mourning—all of these are right, healthy, fully Christian responses to death. But where we differ as Christians is that our sadness and tears give way to an inner grace, an inner joy, in the assurance that our loved one is with God.

The prayer of the church from the funeral mass says it beautifully: "In him who rose from the dead, our hope of resurrection dawns. The sadness of death gives way to the bright promise of immortality. Lord, for your faithful people life is changed, not ended. When the body of our earthly dwelling lies in death, we gain an everlasting dwelling place in heaven."

EIGHT

We Are the Lord's

H EALTH AND SICKNESS, healing and suffering,
death and resurrection: in this book I have tried
to speak to all aspects of a Christian understanding of
sickness and healing.

Health and physical strength and vitality are wonderful gifts. From the beginning God intended us to
enjoy these gifts; we experience them even now as
signs of his mercy and blessing. As I have said so often
in this book, it is right that we seek health and
strength, that we ask God for healing, that we fight
against sickness and affliction.

Yet physical health is not the most important gift
God can give us. The greatest gift we can receive in this
life is to know the Lord himself.

"I have come to rate all as loss in the light of the
surpassing knowledge of my Lord Jesus Christ,"
wrote the apostle Paul. "I wish to know Christ and the
power flowing from his resurrection; likewise to know
how to share in his sufferings by being formed into the
pattern of his death" (Phil 3:8,10). Paul willingly took
on great hardships and suffering in his ministry,
because he knew that comfort and health and life itself

counted as nothing compared to the joy of knowing the Lord Jesus Christ.

In this respect the Christian view of health and sickness, healing and suffering, has little to do with the current craze of body worship. We do not measure the value of our lives by our health or beauty or the size of our muscles. We are valuable because God loves us, and his love remains constant whether we are sick or healthy, full of faith or full of doubts, physically beautiful or physically deformed. It is his love that sustains us in every kind of difficulty or suffering.

"We are afflicted in every way possible, but we are not crushed," wrote Paul. "Full of doubts, we never despair. We are persecuted but never abandoned; we are struck down but never destroyed. Continually we carry about in our bodies the dying of Jesus, so that in our bodies the life of Jesus may also be revealed. . . . We do not lose heart, because our inner being is renewed each day even though our body is being destroyed at the same time" (2 Cor 4:8-10,16).

It is our inner being that will never die, that will never get old or worn out. When we experience the Lord's power to heal our bodies, it is only a sign of his far greater power to renew our inner selves so that we can share life with him forever.

"Indeed," Paul continues, "we know that when the earthly tent in which we dwell is destroyed we have a dwelling provided for us by God, a dwelling in the heavens, not made by hands but to last forever" (2 Cor 5:1).

Whenever we turn to the Lord to ask for healing, we are motivated first of all by the simple desire to escape suffering and loss. There is nothing wrong with that.

In fact, I believe God put that desire for health and well-being in our hearts.

Yet as we grow closer to the Lord in love and faith and prayer, another motivation also grows in us: a desire to serve the Lord and accomplish his will, even at the cost of our own health and well-being. This has profound implications for the way we pray for healing. More and more, we pray not simply to be delivered from sickness and suffering for ourselves but to be healed so we can better serve the Lord, so that we can fulfill the responsibilities he has given us, so that we can proclaim his love to others. And if we do not experience physical healing, we pray that God will work through our sickness and suffering to accomplish his will in us and in others.

"None of us lives as his own master and none of us dies as his own master," writes Paul. "While we live we are responsible to the Lord, and when we die we die as his servants. Both in life and in death we are the Lord's" (Rom 14:7-8).

The most important thing in our lives is that we are the Lord's. In health and strength and vigor we are the Lord's. In sickness and suffering and pain we are the Lord's. Whether we are instantaneously and completely healed or must continue to bear affliction, we are the Lord's. Whether we live or whether we die, we are the Lord's.

There is a surrender called for here, a total abandonment of our own will and desires. And we can only make that kind of surrender when we know, absolutely, that God loves us. He loves us in the midst of pain, in the midst of anguish, in the midst of struggle, in the midst of heartbreak. He loves us so much that he took all our pain upon himself.

My prayer for each person reading this book is that
you will come to know the Lord's love for you. I pray
that if you are suffering from illness, you will look for
healing. I know that the Lord in his goodness and love
for you has healing to bestow.

But I also pray that your faith in Jesus Christ will not
waver, that you will not give in to discouragement and
despair and depression. Grab hold of Jesus. Grab hold
of the crucified and risen one. And then, even as you
ask for physical strength and health, you will recognize
his work deep inside, transforming your inner being
and preparing you for the life that will never end.

Then you will find the fullness of the Lord's gift of
healing.

In closing this book I would like to offer a prayer
that can be used in asking the Lord to heal us or our
loved ones. While I have written it as a prayer to be said
on one's own, it is also my prayer for each one of my
readers:

Holy God and Father of all,
you who are the source of health and healing,
you who relieve suffering and comfort the afflicted,
have mercy on me and on my loved ones.
Rescue us from all sickness.
Restore us to that health and vigor which is in
     accord with your will.

Lord Jesus Christ,
you entered our world to vanquish sin and push
     back the power of Satan.
Give me strength to break with every form of sin
     and evil.

Free me from all the oppression and sickness and
    darkness
that sin has brought into my life.
Let me share in your victory
and know even now the joy of your resurrection.

Holy Spirit of God,
pour forth your healing gifts upon your church.
We ask that wonders and signs and miracles and
    healings
be manifested among God's people.
Equip and empower us to heal the sick,
to comfort the sorrowing,
to break every form of oppression.

Even as I turn to you for healing, Lord,
I also offer you all of my own suffering and pain.
I offer it to you, Father,
in union with the suffering of your Son Jesus on the
    cross.
Let my suffering be as a prayer,
not only for me but also for all those who need
    salvation in Christ,
especially my family and those close to me.

In life or in death, Lord,
in strength or in sickness,
I am yours.

Other Books of Interest from Servant Publications

Yielding to the Power of God
The Importance of Surrender, Abandonment, and Obedience to God's Will
Ann Shields

A challenge to Christians to move more deeply into the heart, mind, and spirit of God, and a vision of the consequences of doing so. *$1.95*

Miracles Do Happen
Sister Briege McKenna, O.S.C.
with Henry Libersat

Some people believe in the *theory* of miracles. Sister Briege McKenna believes in the *reality* of miracles because she sees them happen. The story of a healing ministry which has taken Sister Briege all over the world. *$4.95*

Healing Principles
Ten Basic Keys to Successful Prayer
Father Michael Scanlan, T.O.R.

Practical advice and scriptural insights Christians can apply when praying for healing. *$1.95*